CHURCH, MINISTRY, AND SACRAMENTS
IN THE NEW TESTAMENT

The 1983 Didsbury Lectures

CHURCH, MINISTRY,

AND

SACRAMENTS

IN THE

NEW TESTAMENT

C. K. BARRETT

Exeter
The Paternoster Press

AUSTRALIA:
Bookhouse Australia Ltd.,
P.O. Box 115, Flemington Markets, NSW 2129

SOUTH AFRICA
Oxford University Press,
P.O. Box 1141, Cape Town

British Library Cataloguing in Publication Data

Barrett, C.K.
    Church, ministry and sacraments in the New
Testament.
    1. Church—Biblical teaching
    I. Title
    260   BV597

ISBN 0-85364-406-3

Typeset in Great Britain by
Busby's Typesetting & Design, 52 Queen Street, Exeter, Devon
and printed for The Paternoster Press,
Paternoster House, 3 Mount Radford Crescent, Exeter, Devon
by A. Wheaton & Co. Ltd., Exeter, Devon.

Contents

Preface

This small volume contains the Didsbury Lectures, which I delivered at the British Isles Nazarene College, Manchester, in November 1983, and my first duty, a very pleasant one, is to express my thanks to the College for the invitation to give the Lectures and for the kind and friendly hospitality that I received. It was my first encounter with the Church of the Nazarene; I hope it will not be the last.

The subject I chose for the Lectures hardly needs explanation, but my choice of it may do so. During the last twenty or thirty years it has been my lot—unsought, undesired—to spend a good deal of time in debate and controversy touching the unity of the Christian church. It is paradoxical that a Methodist who owes more than he can ever estimate to two Anglo-Catholics (though they had no love for party labels or party positions), Edwyn Hoskyns and Noel Davey, and himself spent thirty-seven years teaching theology under the shadow of Durham Cathedral in close friendship with the best of colleagues, the majority of whom were Anglicans—it is paradoxical, I say, that such a man should bear a fair measure of responsibility for the failure of schemes to unite the Church of England and the Methodist Church. Certainly it has not been the unity of the two churches, but only the kind of unity sought, and the means proposed for achieving it, that have evoked my opposition. And I think that those who have disagreed with me most radically have for the most part recognized that everything that I have said has been based upon the theology of the New Testament and a careful

critical study of the early history of the Christian church—
that is, upon my understanding of New Testament theology,
and my reading of the history. And I may add at once that I
am no more disposed to claim infallibility for myself than to
allow it to any other Christian. I am glad, however, to take
the opportunity of a lull in the debate to set out, in brief
outline, the theology of church, ministry, and sacraments,
and something of their early development, without any controversial intent. This does not mean that I shall escape
controversy. I shall run into it, because the exegetical, theological, and historical problems involved are very difficult
problems, and it is too much to expect that I shall convince
every reader that my solutions of them are correct. Moreover,
it is unlikely that the practical implications of my solutions
(which I do not draw out, still less develop—there was no
time for this in the Lectures) will be acceptable to all. But I
hope that any controversy that does arise will be firmly based
on the only ground on which it can properly be handled, that
is, on the texts in question.

As I prepared the Lectures it was constantly borne in upon
me that I had embarked upon a subject that might perhaps be
reasonably treated in forty-four lectures, but certainly not in
four. I did not draw from this the inference that the attempt
ought not to be made. I think there is a case for setting down
an outline treatment which may be developed later, not
necessarily by myself. It is possible to note at least some of
the cardinal themes and to look at some of the primary New
Testament passages. What is not possible is to conduct a
running discussion with others who have treated the same
subject. This I do not greatly regret, not because I have learnt
nothing from others—I have learnt a very great deal—but
because, as I have said, I hope as far as possible to avoid controversy, and at the same time to concentrate on the primary
rather than the secondary sources. The reader must understand that what he has here is a sketch, no more.

I have written, as I tried to speak, in such a way as to be
understood by those who lack an elaborate technical equip-
ment in theology. From time to time readers will find words
transliterated from one of the ancient languages, but they are
always translated, either immediately or in the near context.

CHAPTER ONE

From Jesus to the Church

This lecture, and indeed in some measure all four lectures, could be summed up as the assertion of a paradox, and the drawing of an inference from the paradox. The paradox will appear in different forms; here as the proposition that in the New Testament the church is at the same time central and peripheral. The inference is that those who would understand and interpret the church, and the church itself as it seeks to understand and interpret its own being, fall into error when they neglect one or other limb of the paradox. It will take us all the time we have to work this out.

It would be easy, deceptively easy, to treat it in a very simple way. If you look for the word *ekklēsia* (church) in a New Testament concordance you will find that it is very patchily distributed. In the gospels it occurs hardly at all: never in Mark, never in Luke, never in John, and three times only in Matthew, and those three times in two verses (which later we shall study). In Paul, on the other hand, it occurs frequently: thirty-nine times in Romans, 1 and 2 Corinthians, and Galatians—to go no further. This might be taken to mean that for Paul the church was a concept central to his thought and of great importance, whereas Jesus (or, it might be safer to say, the evangelists) had no interest in it. This conclusion, however, would be so simple, so excessively

simple, as to be misleading. There are other words: *mathētes*
(disciple), for example. Here the proportions are more than
reversed: seventy-three times in Matthew, forty-six times in
Mark, thirty-seven times in Luke, seventy-eight times in
John, a total of 234 times; and not one occurrence in Paul.
These figures are not helpful, but only serve as an example of
the inadequacy of word-study conducted on simplistic lines.

Consider the opening chapters of Mark. Commentators do
not agree on the number of verses that may be described as
Mark's introduction to his book. Some stop at v.8, some go
on to v.13; I think that (though it is very unlikely that Mark
thought in the same way that we do about Introductions and
Prefaces) the first fifteen verses must be reckoned as a preliminary setting of the scene. First, there is the title that tells
us what we are to read about: "Beginning of the Gospel of
Jesus Christ"; then John the Baptist, who must be there, not
only to provide a background that will place Jesus in the
world of religion but also to indicate that we have now
reached the last page of the Old Testament—and of the
Apocrypha, if your Bible contains that section. Then Jesus is
baptized, an event recorded not only because it happened
but—and, I think, much more—for its christological significance: Jesus is the one to whom God said, "Thou art my Son,
the beloved." If Jesus is God's Son, what will he do? Fight the
devil, in God's name; so the temptation comes next. And if he
is God's Son, what will he say? "The time is fulfilled, the
kingdom of God has come near; repent and believe in this
good news." This bare sentence is not, and was never intended by Mark to be, the utterance of a particular occasion. It
is the conviction that Jesus stood for, the proclamation that
makes sense of his life. So far, apart from the baptism, which,
as I have said, stands where it does less as an event than as a
christological definition, we have had no incidents but a
thematic introduction to the book as a whole. The first event
follows, and it is the calling of disciples (Mark 1:16-20). Jesus'
first act in his ministry, as Mark narrates it, is to associate
with himself, as potential fishers of men, the two pairs of
brothers, Simon and Andrew, James and John. From this
point onwards disciples are never far away, and in the
opening chapters of his gospel Mark is at pains to make clear

that they form an indispensable element in the work of Jesus. There is neither time nor need to collect every reference. We hear of the call of Levi (2:14); we learn that there were many who followed (2:15); we hear—negatively at least—of their habits: they do not fast as the Pharisees and the disciples of John do, that is, they do not belong to any of the pious groups (2:18). Mark tells us that Jesus picked twelve out of a larger group, for two purposes—that they might be with him, and that he might send them out (3:14). The first of these purposes may be less dramatic than the second but it is no less important. The first task of the disciples is simply to exist, to exist in relation to Jesus. I do not press the point, but I suspect that Mark had one piece of tradition about the Twelve and that he split it in two. In 6:7-13 he left the piece about the commissioning and mission of the Twelve, but cut off from it, and placed at an earlier point, the piece about their appointment. If he did this, it must have been in order to emphasize that from the beginning Jesus associated this group with himself.

Of their importance there is no question. Consider one of the most difficult passages in the gospel, 4:11f.: "To you has been given the mystery of the kingdom of God, but to those who are outside all things come in parables, in order that however hard they look they may not see, however hard they listen they may not understand." Who are "those who are outside"? They are contrasted with those who have asked the question about the parables to which Jesus is here replying: these are *hoi peri auton syn tois dōdeka*, those who were about him with the Twelve. The Twelve are mentioned here because (after 3:13-19) they form the clearest example of what Mark has in mind. *Hoi peri auton* are "his party", those who are on his side. Mark has carefully prepared the way for his description of the two groups, *hoi exō* (those who are outside) and *hoi peri auton*, by telling at the end of chapter 3 the story of the coming of the mother and brothers of Jesus. They stand outside, *exō*, summoning him. But they think him mad (3:21), and Jesus' only answer is to look at those around him, *peri auton*, and to say, "Whoever shall do the will of God, he is my mother and sister and brother." The qualification of the disciples, which enables them to understand the

parables, is not superior intelligence; it is personal loyalty,
personal attachment, to Jesus. It is this attachment that Jesus,
in God's name, seeks. It is well known that the word *basileia*,
like the Hebrew and Aramaic *malkût*, does not mean kingdom in the sense of territory or persons ruled over; it means
the action of the king in ruling. But it is true also that this
kingship cannot operate in a vacuum; it is as men accept it
that it is realized.

The gathering of a community, pledged to obey the will of
God as he himself declared it, was thus (according to Mark) a
fundamental element in the work of Jesus; and a group
gathered about and dependent on Jesus, committed to his
understanding of God and of his purpose, is certainly not far
off "church" whether or not the word *ekklēsia* is used to
describe it. There is more to say about this and we must try to
discover it; but for the moment we may say that we have disposed of one over-simplification of the initial paradox. The
other can be disposed of more quickly.

Paul, as I have pointed out, uses the word *ekklēsia* frequently. Yet was there ever such an individualist? It is
inevitable that we should begin with the evidence of
Galatians. Here is an apostle who stands on his own. He owes
his vocation to no human origin; no one—except God—
bestowed apostleship upon him. Nor was he taught the
Gospel. He did not take it over from someone else; it came to
him, Paul, by direct revelation from Jesus Christ. His actions
after this personal, individual commissioning corresponded
to his call. He did not go up to Jerusalem to consult the
authorities there, but set off on his own independent mission
work. Eventually he paid a short visit to Peter and James;
later, again as the result of a revelation made to him personally, he went up to Jerusalem for a more formal discussion
of the scope and methods of the Christian mission. After this,
when trouble arose at Antioch, he alone resisted the rest
when, in his view, they went wrong: Peter, Barnabas, all the
Jewish Christians—he stood up to the whole company and
insisted on his own understanding of the Gospel. And he
makes clear where it all began: "The life I now live in the flesh
I live by faith in the Son of God who loved me and gave himself for me" (2:20); "Henceforth let no one trouble me; I bear

branded in my body the marks of Jesus" (6:17).

All this is in Galatians, and some, considering the historical context of the epistle, might say that this evidence hardly counts. The circumstances were such that Paul was here obliged to speak and act as *Athanasius contra mundum*. Elsewhere, circumstances and his reaction would be different. It can be readily acknowledged that there is a difference in degree between Galatians and the other epistles, but the difference is not qualitative. It is the same man who writes in the relatively uncontroversial Romans. He is called to act as an apostle, set apart (*aphōrismenos*) for the Gospel (1:1). He yearns for the salvation of the Jewish people and clearly sees himself as playing a particular part in their salvation, almost as a new Moses (9:1-3; 10:1; cf. Exod. 32:32). He has personally completed the evangelization of a great part of the Mediterranean world and has a unique role as a pioneer missionary (15:20). There is no need to write more, though it would be easy to go on through the other epistles. Paul, who was constantly at work founding churches and bearing the pastoral burden that they laid upon him (2 Cor. 11:28, "the care of all the churches"), was himself an individualist, and was concerned about the way in which the Gospel impinged upon individuals in his churches (e.g. Phil. 4:2, "I ask Euodia and I ask Syntyche . . .").

So far we have been clearing the ground. If my initial paradox—that the church is both central and peripheral in the New Testament—is to be maintained it cannot be on the ground that whereas some parts of the New Testament, some New Testament writers, thought it important, others were relatively uninterested. If there is truth in the paradox it is to be found at a deeper level. There is no part of the New Testament that does not attach some kind of significance to the fellowship of the followers of Jesus; but there is at the same time something provisional, temporary, penultimate, about who they are and what they do. I have chosen my adjectives carefully—provisional, temporary, penultimate. They are related to the basic situation, which also constitutes the essential paradox, of the church.

The fact is that the church is an eschatological monster, or prodigy, baffling description and definition. There is no difficulty in defining Israel, the people of God, in the Old Testament. There are indeed many historical problems, which this is no place to discuss, but we recognize at once the story of a historical phenomenon: the expanding family of Abraham, who himself migrates from Mesopotamia into Canaan, and whose descendants migrate from Canaan into Egypt. They leave Egypt and receive a legal constitution under Moses; this makes them a people. The rest of the story (though full of religious and theological significance) can be told in social, political, and military terms: organization under judges, then under a monarchy; military and economic prosperity followed by military and economic disaster; a division into two parts and the disappearance of one of them; a period of exile, and a return from exile; a long subjection, broken by occasional moments of nationalist success, under various world powers. All this story, and the underlying social organization of the people concerned, though often very difficult in detail, is in essence very simple.

Again, it is not difficult to imagine the final state of the people of God in heaven. It is no part of my intention to describe in these lectures things that eye has not seen nor ear heard. All I am saying at this point is that it is possible to conceive what we have not experienced: a life freed from the limitations of space and time, a life of uninterrupted and uninhibited communion with God, a life in which the elect receive, individually and collectively, the fullness of life for which they were created. "Therefore are they before the throne of God, and serve him day and night in his temple: and he that sitteth on the throne shall dwell among them. They shall hunger no more, neither thirst any more: neither shall the sun light on them, nor any heat. For the Lamb which is in the midst of the throne shall feed them, and shall lead them unto living fountains of waters: and God shall wipe away all tears from their eyes" (Rev. 7:15-17). That we are obliged to use pictorial language no more denies the reality of this people of God than the fact that in dealing with the people of God in the Old Testament we are obliged to speak as historians and use social and political categories.

But what of the church, which is neither the one of these things nor the other? This is what I mean when I speak of it as an eschatological monster, historical and not historical, eschatological and not eschatological, and use the adjectives provisional, temporary, penultimate. It exists "between the times", between the straightforward historical past of Israel according to the flesh, and the infinite future of the saints in heaven. We can pursue this question if we turn, as it is clear that sooner or later we shall be obliged to do, to the Matthean passages in which the word *ekklēsia* occurs.

Matt. 18:17 occurs in a passage dealing with community discipline. "If your brother sins against you, go and rebuke him between yourself and him alone. If he listens to you, you have gained your brother. If he does not listen to you, take with you one or two more, that 'at the mouth of two or three witnesses every matter may be established.' If he does not listen to them, tell it to the *ekklēsia*; and if he does not listen to the *ekklēsia*, let him be to you as a Gentile or a tax-collector (18:15-17). It has often been said that in this passage *ekklēsia* means nothing more than a local community—indeed (as the choice of "'Gentile and tax-collector" as a repre-sentative description of an outsider shows) a local Jewish community, or synagogue. Linguistically then, *ekklēsia* will be the equivalent of the Hebrew *keneset*, or the Aramaic *kᵉništa*. In the sense that we are here dealing with a body of limited size exercising discipline over its members, and capable therefore of excluding those whose membership it is not prepared to tolerate, this is undoubtedly true. But two things are to be said about this. One is self-evident: the Christian context in which Matthew took shape was a society that did exist in this form; the evangelist knew communities that existed in this form and practised this kind of discipline. The second is that, although this local meaning gives the principal sense of the passage before us, it is most unlikely that the evangelist would have used in chapter 18 the word *ekklēsia* without recalling the sense in which he had used the word in chapter 16. This is part of the very important fact (unfortunately obscured by the *New English Bible*) that the New Testament uses the same word to denote both the local Christian community and the *ecclesia catholica*, the whole company of God's people. We now have to ask how the word is used in chapter 16 and to what circle of ideas it introduces us.

The words are among the most famous in the gospels: "Blessed are you, Simon Barjonah, for flesh and blood did not reveal it [my Messiahship] to you, but my Father who is in heaven. And I for my part say to you that you are Peter (*Petros*), and on this rock (*petra*) I will build my *ekklēsia*, and the gates of Hades shall not prevail against it" (16:17,18).

The historicity of this saying has evoked a whole library of controversial literature, much of which is related to Roman Catholic claims and Protestant counter-charges and has little to do with serious historical criticism. It is difficult, and indeed mistaken, to separate the issues of historicity and interpretation, for each turns upon the other. If, for example, in this verse *ekklēsia* is taken to mean the World Council Secretariate in Geneva, with the Roman Curia thrown in for good measure, we may be quite confident that Jesus did not utter it. Of course no one would go to such an extreme of absurdity. What does the verse refer to? Its content must be analysed.

(a) The fundamental image is drawn from building; and this is already familiar in Judaism, not least in Jewish eschatology, which sometimes looks to the provision by God in the last days of a new, or renewed, Temple. The theme is reflected in the tradition of the teaching of Jesus. He was alleged to have said, "I will destroy this Temple that is made with hands and in three days I will build another, not made with hands" (Mark 14:58; cf. 15:29; also John 2:19). It is perhaps more than coincidence that 1 Peter 2:5 uses the same image. On the Jewish side it may suffice to quote the fourteenth of the Eighteen Benedictions (an ancient part of the Synagogue liturgy): "To Jerusalem, thy city, return in mercy, and dwell therein as thou hast spoken; (re)build it soon in our days as an everlasting building, and speedily set up therein the throne of David. Blessed art thou, O Lord, who (re)buildest Jerusalem *(bôneh yeruš^elaim)*." The building of course is significant on account of those who live in it, and the prayer (like other passages that I do not quote) contemplates the existence of a renewed people of God living in a rebuilt city and worshipping in a rebuilt Temple. That is, the Matthaean passage makes us think of the eschatological people of God living at and after the End.

(b) The Matthaean building is founded on a person. This is the plain interpretation of the words, and no other is plausible. If they were originally spoken in Aramaic (where the word for rock, *kēpā*, is identical with the name, latinized and anglicized as Cephas) it is certain. This use of the image occurs in the Old Testament (Isa. 51:1f.; the old Israel was founded upon Abraham), and is found several times in the New Testament. At Rev. 21:14 the holy city is said to have twelve foundations, and these bear the names of the twelve apostles of the Lamb. At Eph. 2:20 the church of the saints is said to be built upon the foundation of the apostles and prophets. A similar image is used at Gal. 2:9, where three persons, James, Cephas, and John, are described as pillars—primary supports of a building. It is a somewhat different image when Jesus himself is said to be the only possible foundation (1 Cor. 3:11; 1 Peter 2:5f.). When men are the foundation the sense is that which we have in mind when we speak of foundation members of a society; that is, in Matthew, Peter, in virtue of his confession of faith, is taken to be the first member of the *ekklēsia*. This does not in itself mean that he was or was to be its leader or head, though it is consistent with such a position. It is worth noting that the next verse (about binding and loosing) is an individualizing of what is said in 18:18 to a group; the same may well be true of 16:18. Among a number who were in at the beginning Peter came first.

(c) The *ekklēsia* thus founded is assured of divine protection: the gates of Hades shall not prevail against it. These are the forces of the underworld in general, Satan and his minions; or perhaps, particularly, the power of death (cf. 1 Cor. 15:26). In either case the sense will be not that the church will stand unharmed while age after age of secular history is unrolled, but that the eschatological community will weather the storms of the last days, the last desperate attacks of evil before the End.

(d) The original setting and meaning of the saying were probably that the little flock collected by Jesus, with Peter's name as the first in the list, would survive till the age to come. Compare Mark 9:1: "There are some of those standing here who shall not taste death till they see the kingdom of God

come in power." Also 13:20: "If the Lord had not shortened
the days no one would have come safely through, but for the
sake of the elect whom he chose he did shorten the days." But
the context shows a process of de-eschatologization, neces-
sitated by the fact that the *ekklēsia* found that it was obliged
to go on living in this world. So Peter (16:19) and his
colleagues (18:18) are given a quasi-rabbinic authority to
bind and loose, that is, to forbid certain things and to permit
others. The same process may well apply to the power of the
keys (16:19), and we may recall our earlier notice of the use
of *ekklēsia* in 18:17. The kingdom of the saints of the Most
High, which belongs to the end of time, turns out to look like
the local synagogue; and a particular *keneset* of Jewish
Christians, Christian Jews, finds that its proper home is in
heaven, where alone its true meaning will appear. This is
what I mean when I say that the New Testament church is a
kind of eschatological monster, neither one thing (of the
present) nor the other (of the future). And I add at once, lest
my perhaps unfortunate word be misunderstood, a monster
intended and brought into being by God. Like Paul, the
church as a whole was (and is) an abnormality, an untimely
birth, a freak, an *ektrōma* (1 Cor. 15:8). If the story had
ended with the ascension of Jesus and, with this, the assumption into heaven of the elect, there would have been no
problem; but it did not end there.

We must search in the New Testament for further information about the church, and, at this stage in the discussion,
about its theological definition. The church has often been
described as an "extension of the incarnation". This is not a
theologically satisfactory term. It is perhaps fair enough to
use it in a paraenetic sense: as Christ's physical body was at
his disposal during his earthly, incarnate ministry, so the
members of his body the church should be at his disposal for
service now. But as a theological definition it obscures the
necessary distinction between the head and the members, the
kyrios and his *douloi*, the Redeemer and the redeemed. To
say this is not to deny the close relation between Christ and
the church; I should however prefer to speak of the church as
a function of christology. This can be quickly illustrated by a
glance at the christological terminology used in the New

Testament. Thus a primary term is the word Christ itself, which goes back to the Hebrew *māśiah*, Messiah; the New Testament presents the view that Jesus was the anointed king of Israel, the people of God. A king is nothing without a people over whom to rule; this platitude, perspicuous in itself, is nowhere clearer than in the Old Testament, where king and people are intimately united. The king's charismatic virtue is for his people's benefit; if he sins, not only he but the people also will suffer. Jesus is set forth as greater than David, greater than Solomon, but he shares with them this representative character. Jewish eschatology knows not only the anointed king of the last days but also the anointed priest. In this role Jesus is even more clearly and significantly a representative figure.

A particularly striking example is to be found in the description of Jesus as the one seed of Abraham, in Galatians 3. Paul's curious linguistic argument is familiar: the Old Testament text speaks not of *spermata* ("seeds", plural), but of *sperma* ("seed", singular). Paul knew as well as any modern student of Greek that *sperma* is a collective noun; it could not possibly have been used in the plural, and Paul duly makes his point in 3:29: You (plural) are the seed (collective) of Abraham—if you belong to Christ. He is the one seed in whom the collective seed exists, the realization of the obedient faith which characterizes Abraham as the father of the race.

Similar observations could be made about the two most significant christological descriptions. As Son of God, Jesus is the first-born, the eldest among a large company of brothers (Rom. 8:29). Doubtless we shall have to say that their sonship differs from his, yet it is dependent on and thus related to his. Their sonship could not exist apart from his, but his would not be complete apart from theirs. As Son of man Jesus is the completely representative man; not a representative of the Jewish people alone (as "Messiah" and "seed of Abraham" might suggest) but of the whole human race. "Son of man" is used in the gospels in a variety of ways, but almost always in relation to others. It is not itself a collective term, but it implies a collectivity. If the Son of man is to suffer, he will give his life as a ransom for many; if he is

to come in glory, he will come in order to gather together his
elect (Mark 10:45; 13:27).

Edwyn Hoskyns, in *Essays Catholic and Critical* (ed. E.G.
Selwyn; London, S.P.C.K., 1926), may have exaggerated
somewhat but he was not far wrong when he wrote: "For the
Catholic Christian *'Quid vobis videtur de Ecclesia, What
think ye of the Church?'* is not merely as pertinent a question
as *'Quid vobis videtur de Christo, What think ye of the
Christ?'*: it is but the same question differently formulated"
(p. 153). Say *Christ,* and one way or another you have
implied the existence of *church.* But we have still a long way
to go. I said that the church may be regarded as a function of
christology; this means that the church may be regarded as
the function of a theological proposition—for that is what
christology is. That may be a valid theological observation,
but it leaves not merely unanswered but unasked a historical
question. Given that the church is a function of christology,
may it also be described as a function of the historical Jesus?
In other words—the question is not a new one—what sort of
continuity, if any, exists between the historical Jesus and the
historical church? Is there on the plane of history anything
that corresponds to the theological relation between Christ
and the church, which we have already briefly considered? It
is much easier to be content with the theological relation. The
historical problem is a very difficult one, and it is made no
easier by the ready assumption (which we all tend to make)
that we know, as it were by instinct, a good deal about the
historical Jesus and even more about the historical church.
But in the study of the Bible there is no greater mistake than
to divorce theology from history, history from theology, and
there is an Apollinarian heresy of the church just as there is
an Apollinarian heresy in christology; the historic reality of
the community must be maintained as much as the historic
reality of the manhood. To forget either is not to enhance but
to depreciate the superhuman aspect of each. This is a matter
which a glance into the history of New Testament scholarship
may illuminate.

At the beginning of this century the two most notable
figures (as we see now, with the privilege of hindsight to help
us) were William Wrede and Albert Schweitzer. Each of them

has given us a phrase—and much more than a phrase—that is still in use. Wrede did not invent the "Messianic Secret" (it might be nearer the truth, though not quite the truth, to say that Mark invented it) but he made the phrase and the fact inescapable and unforgettable. Why, in the gospels and especially in Mark, does Jesus appear so concerned not to publicize his messianic status but rather to keep it secret? Commands to the healed not to report their cures, to Peter not to make his confession of messiahship known, and so on, are common: why? In a word, Wrede's answer was that during his ministry Jesus was not, was not thought to be, was not said to be, the Messiah. He did not represent himself in this light, no one saw him in this light. Only after he was believed to have been raised from the dead did men begin to believe that he had in fact been God's Chosen One. Here for the church, when eventually it evolved belief in his messiahship, was a problem: How could Jesus have been Messiah without being known to be Messiah? The church hit upon the theory that Jesus had indeed been the Messiah but had not wished to be known as Messiah till after his crucifixion and resurrection. That he had not been recognized as Messiah was his own inscrutable choice; the secret was his own secret, and he had kept it well. The theory was canonized in Mark's gospel, but it did not go back to Jesus himself; it was a piece of early Christian theologizing.

This was perhaps the first absolutely plain statement of the view that the tradition we have in the gospels was not historically but theologically determined; its concern was not to present a correct historical picture of a historical figure, Jesus of Nazareth, but to present this person in a theological role and incidentally to explain why he had not been recognized in that role during his lifetime. This last was a historical fact; the tradition as the church transmitted it was concerned to cover up the fact by explaining it away. So far as Wrede is right, the gospels are theological documents, and any history they may contain is overlaid with theology and cannot be seen until the theology is cleared away.

Schweitzer's classic account of attempts to write the life of Jesus has, in its English translation, given us another phrase that can stand beside the "Messianic Secret". This is the

"Quest of the Historical Jesus"—so telling a phrase that it has been perpetuated since Schweitzer's time in the so-called *New Quest of the Historical Jesus*. The two phrases, Messianic Secret and Quest of the Historical Jesus, may well stand side by side since, as is well known, Schweitzer considered that the only possible alternative to Wrede's radical scepticism was his own thorough-going eschatology. It was, he believed, possible to get at a historical tradition about Jesus, to find the historical Jesus who had escaped the historians of the eighteenth and nineteenth centuries. Jesus had believed in and proclaimed the coming of the kingdom of God. He knew that its coming must be preceded by the messianic affliction, through which the people of God must pass before entering upon the good time to come; and to force its coming, and to spare his followers, he went to Jerusalem to engineer his own death, absorb the affliction in his own person, and precipitate the final crisis. He succeeded in bringing about his own death, but not the coming of the kingdom. He pinned his faith to an apocalyptic timetable, and it failed him. 'The wheel [of the world] rolls onward, and the mangled body of the one immeasurably great Man, who was strong enough to think of Himself as the spiritual ruler of mankind and to bend history to His purpose, is hanging upon it still. That is His victory and His reign" (*The Quest of the Historical Jesus*, E.T., London, A. & C. Black, 1936; p. 369).

There is both truth and error in Schweitzer's reconstruction. For the present I have only one point to note. Wrede saw the church, as it transmitted traditions about Jesus, as operating theologically upon an untheological story; Schweitzer saw the story itself as theological, and took Jesus to be the first theological interpreter of his own ministry. For Schweitzer, Jesus' own interpretation was theologically unacceptable; it was impossible to believe it because the crucial event that would have made sense of it all had not happened: the kingdom had not come in power as the immediate sequel to the Passion. Not only was Jesus himself mistaken; he was working with concepts that we do not and cannot use. The stars did not fall out of heaven in the year 30, and very few of us can persuade ourselves that they are likely to do so before the end of 1983. What we may—and, I think, must—take

from Wrede and Schweitzer, what New Testament scholarship has in fact taken from them, is the recognition that the
tradition is theological all through. Students will differ in the
amount of historical information about Jesus of Nazareth
that they believe can be won from the gospels, but they will,
on the whole, agree that both Jesus and the later bearers of
the tradition about him understood what they were doing,
and what they were talking and writing about, in theological
terms. This is a fact that makes it difficult both to unearth the
history and to present the theology in a neat systematic form;
but it is nonetheless a fact, and the more inconvenient a fact
may at first appear to be the more important it is to recognize
it, remember it, and wrestle with it.

I have evoked Wrede and Schweitzer, those grandfathers
of modern New Testament scholarship, partly in order to
make the point that both in the study of Jesus and in the
study of the church which looked back to him, it is important
to keep equally in play both lines, the historical and the
theological, but also for another reason. They will serve to
introduce a very familiar quotation from one more or less
their contemporary, to whom also we are greatly indebted,
Alfred Loisy. Probably the best known sentence in his
voluminous works is: "Jesus foretold the kingdom, and it was
the Church that came" (*The Gospel and the Church*, E.T.,
London, Isbister, 1903; p. 166). This puts Schweitzer's
dilemma in epigrammatic form, and, if it is the whole truth, it
means that the church cannot be regarded as a function of the
historical Jesus. He was looking for the reign of God in new
heavens and a new earth, where human beings would be as
the angels in heaven; what came into being after his death
was a miscellaneous group of men and women, living human
lives on this earth, still mortal, still sinful, formulating their
common life in a variety of ways, which arose to a great
extent out of social conditions and in conformity with sociological principles.

I have no intention of discussing here the very difficult
question what Jesus looked for in the future. I have written
about it elsewhere and shall be content with two or three
propositions from which few, I believe, are likely to dissent. I
see no evidence in the gospels that Jesus looked forward to a

continuous life of the church in this world, extending through at least nineteen and a half centuries and still showing no sign of coming to an end. I see a little evidence that suggests that he may have contemplated a short period—perhaps a single generation—in which his followers would wait for the climax to come. I see a good deal of evidence that points to an unshakable conviction that suffering and death lay ahead of him, but that after obedient suffering God would certainly vindicate him. This conviction was expressed in terms that had already become familiar in apocalyptic literature— resurrection and parousia, both waiting, for example, to be developed out of the book of Daniel (for the resurrection of the martyred righteous teachers see 12:2f.; for a picture which could be developed into the notion of a coming Son of man see 7:13f.). In fact—and here at least there will be no dispute—the resurrection happened; the parousia did not; so that the followers of Jesus were left in a period they had not expected, or at least had not expected to last long, a period of what we may allow ourselves to describe as partially realized eschatology.

In this period they had to extemporize a good deal. How they did this in some important respects I shall be discussing in the second and third lectures. Here I may take an example that has been fully worked out by J. Jeremias, in *Jesus' Promise to the Nations* (E.T., London, S.C.M., 1958). What had Jesus to offer to the Gentiles? To judge from the gospels, very little. He hardly spoke to a Gentile; and if he could compliment a gentile centurion ("I have not found so great faith, no, not in Israel"; Matt. 8:10; Luke 7:9) he could speak rough words to a Syrophoenician woman ("It is not a good thing to take the children's bread and throw it to the dogs"; Mark 7:27). There are hints, in a few parables, and in apocalyptic discourses. Here, as Jeremias has shown, is the clue. Jesus shared the view of a few Old Testament prophets that at the End the Gentiles would flock to the mountain of the Lord's house. The God of Israel would have room for them, but only in the age to come. So what is to be done in the unexpected period between the resurrection and the parousia? In the evidence available we can trace different attitudes in the early church. There were, it seems, those who were content to sit still in Jerusalem and wait for the End to happen: "If the Lord means to save the heathen he will do it without our assistance—and he will do it (if at all) very soon." There were others who took the view that the Gentiles might be accepted but only on Jewish terms; that is, they must be circumcised and required to observe all the regulations of Judaism. There were others again who said, "There is now but one way to God, and it is not the law. It is Jesus, crucified and risen; in him shall the Gentiles trust." And between the various groups there were compromises, such as the Decree of Acts 15:29.

There remains now hardly time enough to do what I ought perhaps to have done at the beginning of this first lecture. I must define the word church. I am using the word in the sense of the *ecclesia visibilis*, the *ecclesia militans*. Using this definition we may begin to see the paradox of a theme which is at once central and peripheral. This church may be described as the church, the people, of the interim. If we consider it as merely filling a little space between the earthly work of Jesus and God's consummation of all history it becomes insignificant, for we are bound to compare it with the *ecclesia triumphans* which in the immediate presence of God expresses to perfection his purpose for humanity. Yet this interim exists, and no Christian theologian will question that it exists by the will of God, whose intention is that his people shall not be wafted immediately to heaven to enjoy eternal bliss but shall share the discipline of life in a vale of weeping and of joy, knowing both the peace and the desolation of faith.

> And now we watch and struggle,
>   And now we live in hope,
> And Zion in her anguish
>   With Babylon must cope.

But it is by leaving them to cope with Babylon that God fits his people for that "sweet and blessed country, the home of God's elect"; so that what at first appears an interlude, peripheral to God's purposes, becomes central and indispensable.

There is another way of looking at the paradox. The people of God is a collection of human beings. Between resurrection and parousia it lives in this world, and therefore shares many characteristic features with a nation state, a university, a cricket club. An association of persons cannot hope to have a stable and permanent existence without some form of organisation; this applies to the church as much as to any other association. In the course of its history it may therefore be expected to pick up, and undoubtedly has picked up, characteristics which are entirely peripheral to its essential nature. Yet at the same time its essential nature, if this is not to be a purely theoretical matter, has to be expressed, and has been expressed, in certain formal characteristics which, because of what they express, are of central importance. So the church, as an organized society, will sometimes appear central and sometimes peripheral to the purpose of God.

The two forms of the paradox are related to each other, though they are not identical. The church as the body that lives under—or indeed on—the cross is expressing in its disciplined and triumphant life the very nature of its Lord; and this is not in any sense peripheral. Yet it is in its Babylonian exile that it acquires such peripheral Babylonian qualities as it uses in expressing the death and life of Jesus (2 Cor. 4:10). Thus it is not that there are some bits of the church that are vital and some that are unessential; every bit shares the twofold character of the whole.

This first lecture has been on the whole a theological discussion, focused upon the relation between the humiliated and glorified Jesus and the humiliated and one day to be glorified church. It leaves us asking the question how this strange, paradoxical society appeared on the stage of history. What did it look like, and how did it display central and peripheral features? These historical questions I shall deal with next in two lectures in which I shall examine the development of the ministry and the use of the sacraments in the New Testament. I hoped to take the account further into the post-apostolic period, but it has proved impossible to do this in the compass of two lectures. The treatment will be primarily historical, though I have already indicated that I consider it a major error in dealing with the New Testament to attempt to hold history and theology apart; I shall try not to commit this error. In the fourth lecture too I shall do my to keep both history and theology in mind as we study the development of the community, looking, as far as time permits, not only at the New Testament but also at some immediately subsequent developments.

CHAPTER TWO

Ministry

The ground we covered in yesterday's lecture was so vast that
it is, I hope, hardly necessary to apologize for a number of
omissions, and for the fact that some topics were treated very
sketchily. Perhaps it will suffice to say that some things are so
important that one is almost obliged to take them for
granted. We considered the question of the relation between
Jesus and the church, and this, whether looked at historically
or theologically, is so difficult a question that it needs a fairly
thorough discussion—indeed, a longer and more detailed
discussion than we had time for. The first members of the
church found themselves in circumstances that neither they
nor anyone else had expected. The Messiah had come, and
instead of triumphing had been cast out and killed. God had
vindicated him, but partially and privately. The question of
John 14:22 must have been asked many times, and long
before John wrote it down: "How is it that you will manifest
yourself to us and not to the world?" Death, if death there
had to be, should have been followed by public vindication
in the sight of all. The death had been public enough; its
horror and disgrace called for adequate compensation.
"Every eye shall see him, even those who pierced him, and all
the tribes of the earth shall lament over him" (Rev. 1:7). But
he did not come with the clouds, and he did not manifest

himself to the world. He was seen by a few men and women, and those his closest followers. The public event was still outstanding, and the believers found themselves in what was neither the old world nor the new, with a very great deal to think out and explain, about their Master and about themselves.

I have now implied the two major omissions of yesterday's lecture. First, the profound conviction on the part of his closest followers that Jesus had been truly dead and was now truly alive. The only explanation of this event that they themselves saw fit to give was in the words, "God raised him from the dead." This is an affirmation that the historian cannot make in his own right. The acts of God are not susceptible of historical inquiry leading to either verification or falsification. There are indeed affirmations that the historian may and must make. He must affirm that those who knew Jesus best were quite certain that after his crucifixion they had seen him alive, not a ghost or imagined apparition, but Jesus himself. They may have been mistaken, but they were prepared to venture everything for their belief. Again, the historian must affirm that neither Jews nor Romans ever produced the body of Jesus. They may not have looked for it, though one would think that to find it would have been the best way to put down an irritating and unwanted movement. If they looked for it, they did not find it. I am aware that I have given no explanation of what seems to have occurred. This is not an omission, now about to be made up. I have given no explanation because there is none to give. Explanations always arise out of the correlation of data, and here there are no data to correlate; only one datum.

The second thing that has to be explicitly added to yesterday's lecture (though it is hardly necessary) is that these disciples, though they had failed badly at the time of the crucifixion and must have been intellectually bewildered by the new turn of events, were moved by a profound and intense personal loyalty to Jesus. Very few of them, perhaps none of the earliest disciples, could be called a theologian. That did not matter. God had revealed himself not to the wise and intelligent but to babes; and he was soon to supply some remarkable theologians to help the babes with the very difficult problems he had set them by his extraordinary and unexpected acts.

I must add one further preliminary point. After describing the curious position of the church and its relation to Jesus I said that we would go on, in more historical vein, to consider what this strange group actually looked like, how it behaved, and what it did. This was so far fair enough; we must keep history and theology close together and not pursue one too long before we turn to the other. But I went on to say that we would conduct our inquiry under the headings of (first) ministry and (then) sacraments. Sacraments we can leave till tomorrow; ministry as a title for the present lecture might suggest that the whole church is to be seen in the ministry, that only ministers matter, and that the laity is relatively insignificant. Nothing could be further from the truth than this. There are signs, some of which we shall be able to look at, that something like what we call "the ministry" was emerging before the end of the New Testament period; but no more then than now was "the ministry" the church (except in the sense that the whole church is the ministry, that all Christians are ministers).

I have used the word *ministry* for several reasons; one that will suffice at this point is that it gives us a plainly visible and reasonably familiar element in church life. We can look out for it in the New Testament, and if we see something of the kind we can relate it to ministries recognisable today. More-over it is undoubtedly true that a number of familiar terms occur in the New Testament—*episkopos* (overseer, or bishop), *presbyteros* (elder, or presbyter), *diakonos* (minister, or deacon) and a few others which have not persisted in the same way. Study of these terms provides us with a kind of yardstick, a means of comparing the New Testament church with the church at other periods; including our own. The same observations will provide a measuring-rod of another kind too. They will show the extent to which the church, in this formative period, came to terms with the fact that it, the assembly of the saints whose headquarters was in heaven and belonged to the age to come, had for the present to live in this world, and was therefore subject to the historical and social pressures to which any group in this world is exposed.

How, in the brief time at our disposal, are we to conduct this inquiry? The sources are too scanty for us to expect much by way of a record of continuous development; our only course is to take soundings here and there, to put down exploratory borings. And it is clear where our bore-holes must be located: Paul, 1 Peter, the Johannine literature, Acts. There is oil (to pursue my metaphor) in each of these fields; we shall exhaust none of them. There are other important sources of information too, both inside and outside the New Testament; these, like other matters, must wait for the fourth lecture, though even there it will not be possible to deal with all of them.

Few will doubt that the Pauline literature is the earliest Christian writing that we have. One view, which I do not hold, of the Epistle of James would put it earlier than the Pauline correspondence; in any case it would contribute little to our study. Paul became a Christian only a short time after the crucifixion; he was in the Christian story very nearly from the beginning, though in the earliest years he may not have been very near to its centre. By the time he wrote his earliest letters (it makes little difference in this inquiry whether we put 1 Thessalonians or Galatians first) he had been a Christian long enough to have fairly well developed ideas of how the church should be (or should not be) organized, and there is little development to be observed. I deliberately exclude the Pastoral Epistles, which, I believe, bear witness to a post-pauline period. I shall deal with them, so far as possible, in the fourth lecture.

The first thing to be said about the ministry in the Pauline epistles is that every member of the church was a minister. It is better to put the matter in this positive way than to say that the Pauline churches had no ministry in the modern sense of the term; that would be nearly but not quite true. It is entirely true to say that every member of the church had, in Paul's view, like every member of the human body, its own function. Eyes, ears, and nose; hands and feet: each performed its own task, each was necessary to the proper functioning of the whole, none could afford to despise any other. Their functions differed, but all were necessary. So with the church. 1 Cor. 12:7,11 must be taken with complete seriousness. To each one (*hekastōi*) is given his own manifestation of the Spirit, with a view to mutual profit . . . all these things the same one Spirit puts into operation (*energei*), distributing individually to each one (*hekastōi* again) as he wills. It is from this point that Paul goes on to develop his image of the body. The same image is used in Romans 12, with similar and explicit stress on diversity of function. As we have many members in one body, and all the members do not have the same function (*praxis*) so we, who are many, are one body in Christ, and severally members of one another (12:4,5). In each of these passages Paul goes on to specify some of the functions that operated in the churches, and it is clear that his interest is in function rather than in office. To one there is given, through the Spirit, a word of wisdom; to another, in accordance with the same Spirit, a word of knowledge; to another faith, in the same Spirit; to another gifts of healing, in the one Spirit; to another the working of miracles, to another prophecy, to another the power to distinguish between spirits, to another various kinds of tongues, to another the interpretation of tongues (1 Cor. 12:8-10). Later in the chapter he begins to list, if not offices at least descriptions of persons who performed functions in the church: apostles, prophets, teachers; but he soon moves back to functions, continuing his list thus: miracles, gifts of healing, gifts of support, gifts of direction, various kinds of tongues (12:28).

It is interesting to note that in Romans 12 the description moves in the opposite direction. First come the functions: prophecy, ministry (*diakonia*, by which he probably means practical service to the needy); then follow participial descriptions of people who do certain things: he who teaches, he who exhorts, he who gives, he who presides (*ho proistamenos*), he who does acts of mercy (Rom. 12:6-8). But it is significant that the participles are used; Paul is thinking of people doing things, not of offices, that is, of recognized places in the community which must be filled, and confer on those who occupy them a special position of responsibility and authority.

As well as these positive pieces of information there are some notable gaps and silences. Thus there appears to have been at Corinth no church treasurer who could be relied on to administer the church's financial affairs. When Paul speaks in 1 Corinthians 16 of his collection for the saints he does not suggest that the church members should hand in their weekly contributions; they set them aside weekly and Paul collects them when he comes. Similarly in 2 Corinthians 8, it is Paul's colleague Titus, with his appointed travelling companions, who actually collects the money. Paul adhered to this method even though it exposed him to the charge of pocketing the proceeds of the collection (2 Cor. 12:16). Even more striking perhaps (for the moral achievement of the Corinthians was not high enough to suggest that they could easily be trusted with others' money) is the apparent absence of anyone to take charge at the Lord's Supper. The scandals described in 1 Corinthians 11 are familiar; one might have expected Paul to say, "Do not start your supper till the leader says the blessing." But he says simply, "Wait for one another." And though the Corinthian assemblies must have been at times a Babel of tongues and prophesyings he can only give his instructions by letter to the prophets and speakers with tongues; there is nothing in 1 Corinthians 14 to suggest that there was any local officer in the Corinthian church to whom Paul could leave it to see that things were done decently and in order.

This absence of local leadership must have been particularly crippling when the church meeting exercised, as Paul urged it to do, judicial functions. Church members, he insisted, must not take each other to pagan courts; the saints (who would later judge angels) could surely manage everyday affairs for themselves (1 Cor. 6:4f.). But in the case where it was necessary for the church to exercise discipline over the man who had taken his father's wife, he can only write, in a piece of Greek whose obscurity bears witness to the awkwardness of the situation, that the church should get together with his spirit (1 Cor. 5:3-5). Had he been in Corinth he would no doubt have taken the chair; in his absence there was no one to take it for him—at least, he says nothing to suggest that there was such a person.

It is true that one verse in the certainly genuine epistles uses words that were later to become designations of ecclesiastical officials. In Phil. 1:1 Paul writes to "all the saints in Christ Jesus who are in Philippi, with the bishops and deacons" (*syn episkopois kai diakonois*; it is interesting that the Greek nouns have no articles, which would have been expected if the bishops and deacons had been as clear-cut a group as the saints; there can however be no question that there is a reference here to two special classes of Christians). I have given the conventional rendering, bishops and deacons, because we have no idea who or what the persons in question were, and it seems better to beg no questions, or rather to beg them in the most obvious possible way. We may guess at the part the bishops and deacons played in the Philippian church, but we can do no more. It is worth while to observe that one of the main purposes of the epistle was to thank the Philippians for the gift they had sent to Paul. We know that at a later stage in Christian history the *diakonoi* were those to whom the care of the poor was entrusted; and there are non-Christian uses of *episkopos* which refer to financial officers. It is possible that the *episkopoi* were those in Philippi who decided that a gift should be sent to Paul and made the money available, and that the *diakonoi* were those who saw to the transmission of the gift. This is perhaps as good a guess as any. At least there is evidence at Philippi, as there is not at Corinth, for the location of some specific tasks (perhaps eleemosynary) in the hands of particular persons; but even at Philippi it is hard to go further than that.

A quick impression is thus of a leaderless mob; but it is a false impression. As long as Paul lived his churches had a remarkably strong leader, who was not content to found societies and leave them to themselves, but kept a close eye on them, writing letters and sending colleagues when he could not visit them himself, well aware of an authority that had been committed to him with his apostleship. It was a positive authority, "for building you up and not for casting you down" (2 Cor. 10:8; 13:10), but that meant an authority to do precisely what he was commissioned to do, and in order to build it might sometimes be necessary to clear the ground by the casting down of strongholds (2 Cor. 10:4). He did not hesitate to give instructions in his letters, and could promise to set other matters in order when he was able to pay a visit (1 Cor. 11:34); and he might find himself obliged to come with a rod in his hand (1 Cor. 4:21).

Paul had assistants who travelled with him, joined him in writing letters, and could be sent on their own to carry out tasks that Paul would have done had it been possible for him to be in several places at once. He could refer to them as apostles (1 Thess. 2:7) He commended them; he expected them to be well treated and respected (1 Cor. 16:10). There were other travellers who, though they were not, like Silvanus, Timothy, or Titus, members of the team, must have contributed to the success, and to the order and organization, of the mission: Aquila and Priscilla, Stephanas, Fortunatus, and Achaicus, Phoebe and Chloe, among others. They brought messages, and sometimes gifts; they conveyed news; they helped and were helped.

Such people were, notwithstanding the general mobility possible in the settled years of the Empire, in a minority. What of the local churches? and of the functions of which I spoke earlier? How far was the universal ministry of every member organized and distributed?

I have spoken several times of functions. Some would say that we should speak not of functions (though we may recall that Paul does use—in Rom. 12:4—the word *praxis*) but of *charismata*, gifts of divine grace, operated by the Holy Spirit, and bestowed upon individuals in accordance with no human scheme but simply as the Spirit directs (*kathōs bouletai*, 1 Cor. 12:11). This is the true ministry, in which every member shares. It is of divine origin and authority; it is not amenable to human organization; it is spontaneous and free; it is in no sense hierarchical and carries with it only such authority as is inherent in the immediacy of the Spirit's action. I have to say not only that I feel an immediate personal sympathy with this point of view but that I see a good deal of evidence to support it. Paul describes the worship of the church as arising not from a liturgical order but from spontaneously offered contributions springing from the whole company: When you assemble, each one of you has a hymn, a piece of teaching, a revelation, a tongue, an interpretation (1 Cor. 14:26). True, he does not wish too many to speak at once, and plays down the public, community, value of tongues; this modifies but

does not substantially change the picture. Community
services also were done on the basis of gifts. "Helps" and
"governments" (*antilēmpseis* and *kybernēseis*; 1 Cor.
12:28), which it is perhaps possible to connect with the work of
deacons (who helped) and of bishops (who governed), stand
in the same list of spiritual gifts with miracles and tongues. So
does teaching.

So much (for the present) for gifts, *charismata*. There is
also another way of looking at the origins and ground of
ministry. We know from the Pauline letters that gatherings
which Paul calls *ekklēsiai* met in private houses (Rom. 16:5; 1
Cor. 16:19; Phm. 2; cf. Col. 4:15). This means that Aquila
and Priscilla, and at least a few other early Christians, had
houses big enough to hold such groups. In the Empire,
housing conditions were very varied. It is instructive to visit,
for example, such a well preserved collection of domestic and
commercial buildings as the ancient port of Ostia. Here the
comfortable and spacious houses of the prosperous trading
classes stand almost side by side with the *insulae*, great blocks
of flats, in which many families lived in poverty and squalor.
These could not possibly entertain the church. Only the
relatively successful and well-to-do could do this; the poor
would have difficulty enough in accommodating themselves
and their families. Gaius, whom Paul could describe as "my
host, and the host of the whole church" (Rom. 16:23), must
have been a reasonably prosperous man, as was Erastus, the
city treasurer, mentioned in the same verse. The same chapter
(16:1f.) mentions Phoebe, about whom two things are said.
First, she was a *prostatis* "of many, and of me myself". What
does this mean? Greek *prostatis* suggests the Latin *patrona*,
but this she cannot have been in the official, legal sense for
Paul, since he was himself a citizen, and therefore would not
need and could not have such a patron. The word must be
used in a non-technical but nevertheless significant way.
Perhaps she had supported Paul with money, helping to
finance his journeys (which cannot have been cheap), perhaps with social influence; perhaps she had provided legal
assistance. All these things are merely guesses; but one or all
of them, or some similar thing or things must have been true
or Paul could not have used the word he employs. So Phoebe

was a lady of some wealth, standing, and social position. The second thing that Paul has to say about her is that she was a *diakonos* of the church in Cenchreae. So in Cenchreae (one of the ports of the city of Corinth), as in Philippi, they had *diakonoi* (I am not saying that they had anything that we might recognize as an order of deacons), and there was a woman among them. Were Phoebe's social position and her ministry (*diakonia*) in the church totally unrelated? I think not. Imagine a church like that of Corinth, in which there are not many wise, powerful, or nobly born (1 Cor. 1:26). Not many; but a few, a few who have money, education, influence; who are accustomed to leadership, in a business, in the city council; who have large and pleasant houses in which they are prepared to entertain the rag tag and bobtail of the local Christian community. Is there not some probability that these, especially if they came into the church in its early days and have, through long acquaintance with Paul, a good grasp of Christian belief and practice, will gravitate into positions of leadership? It is not snobbery or class-warfare (though these must always have been lurking as potential dangers). It is common sense; it is social inevitability.[1]

In the Pauline churches all the members were equal; but (if one may borrow the phrase) some were more equal than others. There was never a hierarchy; but there were some who were outstanding. A striking example of this occurs in 1 Thessalonians 5. In verse 11 Paul addresses the whole church, bidding all its members exhort one another and build one another up. This, he says, you are already doing (*kathōs kai poieite*), and it represents the mutual ministry which was the foundation of the common Christian life. Addressing the same people, or most of them, in verses 12, 13, he asks them to recognize those who labour among them, preside over them in the Lord, and admonish them. Their fellow members should hold them especially in love on account of the work they do. No official title is supplied; probably there was none to use; but there were in Thessalonica people who stood out among the rest, *primi inter pares*. Paul goes on, once more

---

1. A special study of this matter has been made in a Durham Ph.D. thesis by A.L. Chapple.

addressing the same people, "Admonish [the same word as in verse 12] the disorderly, cheer up the low-spirited, help the weak, be long-suffering with all." He has· returned to the theme of the shared ministry that every Christian owes to every other Christian. This is a perfect cameo of a Pauline church. The churches did not always work as they should have done; Corinth is a notable example of a church running off the rails. But where they functioned properly the churches were full of ministry; and some members were better at it, had greater natural gifts of leadership, than others. It is possible to go further and distinguish three lines along which the mutual service, which all Christians owed to one another but some expressed more adequately than others, moved. After apostles (1 Cor. 12:28) Paul ranks, as servants of the church, prophets and teachers, that is, those who performed the service of the word. Instruction, exhortation, the interpretation of the Old Testament, the word of wisdom and of knowledge, evidently played an important part in the Pauline churches. Paul does not exclude anyone from these forms of service; at the same time it is clear that all did not possess the requisite gifts in the same degree. Higher even than the gift of prophecy was love (e.g. 1 Cor. 13:8). All Christians were expected to love one another (Rom. 13:8-10; Gal. 5:13,14) and to express love in practical terms; again, however, some will have had opportunities denied to others. Third among the kinds of service required of all Christians but performed outstandingly by some was the exercise of discipline. We see this practised by the whole community in 1 Cor. 5:4; but in 1 Cor. 6:5 Paul hopes—it may be in vain— that one wise man may be found to judge between brethren.

It is time to wind up our study of Paul, but the most important thing remains to be said. We have now noted two strong pressures which led to the singling out of some members from among the rest to take leading positions; ministry, though not confined to them, would tend to be concentrated in their hands. One of these was the pressure of religious, and especially of ecstatic experience; the man (or woman) gifted with the power of spiritual speech, whether in his own language or in the language of angels, will naturally wish to be a religious leader, and others will wish him to be one. The other was the pressure of natural ability, strength of personality, and social position. Each of these pressures carried with it a great potentiality of strength for the church; and each carried with it great potential dangers. These are sufficiently evident; church history is full both of the humble and sacrificial service and of the arrogant exercise of power manifested by the spiritually, socially, financially, and intellectually eminent, at whose hands their fellow Christians have received great benefits and suffered great injuries. The New Testament itself is not without examples of both kinds. What remains to be added is that Paul's contribution was to supply the requisite theological factor, necessary if the strength was to be realized and the danger held in check.

Paul did this primarily in relation to himself and the universal ministry which he exercised in all the churches. He could for example speak in tongues more than all the Christians: what an impression he could have made in that sensation-loving church! But he preferred to speak five words with his mind rather than tens of thousands in a tongue in order that he might instruct others and so build up the church (1 Cor. 14:18,19). He might have imposed himself upon the church and lined his pockets at its expense; again, the Corinthians would have been impressed had he done so. He preferred to live in poverty, working with his own hands to keep himself. "Why? Because I do not love you? God knows!" (1 Cor. 9:12; 2 Cor. 11:11; et al). His church members might boast of their religious superiority; he was the sort of apostle who came on last in the show; a spectacle to the whole world (1 Cor. 4:9). The test of spiritual gifts was simple; do they bear witness to the lordship of Christ (1 Cor. 12:3)? The way to give, to use one's worldly resources for the benefit of others, was not merely with liberality but with that simple-mindedness that seeks neither publicity nor reward (*ho metadidous en haplotēti*, Rom. 12:8). The whole, evangelistic preaching and pastoral care, was summed up for him in, "We preach not ourselves but Christ Jesus as Lord (*kyrios*) and ourselves as your slaves (*douloi*), for Jesus' sake" (2 Cor. 4:5).

This is the special Pauline version of the paradox of the church. Its ministry is not merely necessary but inevitable, a

ministry always universal in that every church member parti-
cipates in it, but of growing specialization; yet this specialized
ministry is always denying all the recognized, and usually
desired, accompaniments of leadership, actively subordi-
nating itself to those it could have dominated. The danger I
mentioned at the beginning of the first lecture is clear; a
church that rejects the gifts of leadership will greatly
impoverish itself; a church that allows them to develop in a
worldly way will destroy itself.

The First Epistle of Peter is a post-pauline work. Even if it
was written by the apostle himself it must have been written
towards the close of his life, presupposing the existence both
of the Pauline letter-style and of churches of a Pauline kind
Indeed, if 1 Peter 1:1 is to be taken to mean what it says, it
was written to churches of Pauline foundation. It may imply
persecution such as belongs to the period after Paul's death
(4:12-19), and at first sight it implies also a more developed
ministry. The word *episkopos*, however, was not in use for a
ministerial office. It is hardly likely that God, or Christ,
would be described (2:25) as the "Shepherd and Bishop
(*poimēn kai episkopos*) of your souls" if *episkopos* suggested
the local, or even if it suggested the territorial, minister. But
the word *presbyteros* does appear, and the *presbyteroi* have
clear pastoral functions which they must discharge in a
proper way. "The elders among you I exhort . . . ; shepherd
the flock of God which is among you, not as a matter of
necessity but willingly, in accordance with God's will (*kata
theon*), not for the sake of base gain but eagerly, not as if you
were lording it over the groups allotted to you, but as
examples to the flock" (5:1-3). This passage suggests a state of
things in which a presbyterate has lasted long enough for
some of the perils that beset any ministry to make themselves
felt. The ministry is paid, so that there is a danger that men
may enter it with a view to making money. The ministry has
authority, power, so that there is a danger of the misuse of
power: men may use it so as to impose their will, and themselves, upon their subordinates. The ministry is a job that has
to be done—the church needs ministers, so that there is a
danger that men may be pushed into the ministry without
any true sense of vocation, without, in fact, any vocation at

all. All this, so far, evokes the picture of a settled, presbyterian church.

There is another aspect of the matter. In my quotation from 1 Peter 5:1-3 I omitted some clauses. "The elders among you I exhort, I who am a fellow elder (*sympresbyteros*) and witness of the sufferings of Christ, who am also a partaker in the glory that is to be revealed." The reference is evidently to the apostolic author, whether the epistle was written by Peter himself or is pseudonymous. In what sense could the apostle be described as a *sympresbyteros*? If the author was Peter himself, he could have been modestly ranking himself with those whom he was addressing; like them, he has a pastoral responsibility in the church. If the author was not Peter but was setting out to dignify him, this way of taking the word becomes very improbable. On either view there is a strong, on the latter view a very strong, case for supposing that *presbyteros* has its simple primary meaning of *older man*; Peter then as *sympresbyteros* will simply be saying, I exhort you older people to do as I say; and you may remember that I too am getting on in years. An even stronger ground for seeing an age element in the word *presbyteros* is found in 5:5: *homoiōs, neōteroi, hypotagēte presbyterois*: Similarly (that is, we are dealing with a parallel, converse relationship), you younger men submit yourselves to the—older ones. There is no evidence for *neōteroi* as an order of ministers, and they take the corresponding word *presbyteroi* with them. And if *presbyteroi* in 5:5 are *older men* must they not be *older men* in 5:1 also? So do we after all have a reference here to presbyters (elders), or merely to the older element in the congregation?

This is not a question to which we are obliged to give an exclusive answer. Both elements are present in the text, and the text thus constituted bears witness to an interesting stage in the development of what we call the ministry. It was natural, and there is evidence for it in the Pauline epistles (e.g. 1 Cor. 16:15), that in the earliest years leadership should be exercised by those who had been in the church from the beginning—the "firstfruits". These would tend also to be older in years than the rest; of course, in any individual case this might not be so, but the average age of converts of, say,

thirty years standing would be greater than the average age of
converts of ten years standing. The leaders would thus tend
to be, in a literal sense, *presbyteroi:* older persons. As time
went on, it became clear that age and the quality of leadership were not necessarily correlative, so that quite young men
could become *presbyteroi* (in the sense of leaders), while old
men might be distinguished by no more than a plentiful lack
of wit. 1 Peter has not yet reached that stage; the *presbyteroi*
are not simply older men for they are exercising a ministerial,
pastoral, function (which it is possible for them to exercise
badly). Yet they are, or at least some of them are, old enough
for the group as a whole to be contrasted with the *neōteroi*,
the younger men.

This pastoral ministry operates on the same lines that we
have seen in the Pauline epistles: the Word, loving service,
and discipline. Discipline is the theme of the passage we have
already considered. From 4:12 the author deals with the
severe persecution that has now broken upon the church. It
must be accepted joyfully, but it also calls for discipline. It is
important for the church to tighten up its moral life in order
that it may be clear that, if Christians suffer, it is for the name
of Christ and not because they are guilty of some crime. The
elders, examples to the flock, must play their part here, and
the duty is expressly laid upon them in 5:1-4. The young must
accept the discipline of the old, but all must practise humility.
Be sober; watch. And so the epistle moves to its end.

Earlier (4:11) the other two strands of ministry are
mentioned. If any one speaks, let it be as the oracles of God.
If any one performs service, let it be as of the strength that
God supplies. Speaking and serving are basic community
functions; there is nothing to suggest that they are confined
to special groups of persons: "if *any one* speaks . . . if *any one*
performs service . . . ". It is the whole church that is "built up
as a spiritual house into a holy priesthood, to offer up
spiritual sacrifices"; you (again the whole church) are "an
elect race, a royal priesthood, a holy nation, a people for
God's special possession, to proclaim the excellences of him
who called you out of darkness into his marvellous light"
(2:5,9).

Peter may be a little beyond Paul in his use of *presbyteros;*

but very little. It is not a word Paul uses (notwithstanding
Acts 14:23 and the Pastoral Epistles). It is however one that is
worth noting because it introduces the significant factor of
age. We may imagine a classless society (though none in fact
exists, on either side of the Iron Curtain); we cannot even
imagine one in which there are no age differences. The old
will always tend to tell the young what to do; and the young
will always tend not to do it. Peter does not say that age
makes no difference; he does say that the old must teach by
example and not by making themselves bosses, and that the
younger are to defer to such older ones. Like Paul, he accepts
the given facts—in his case one of the most fundamental and
least avoidable—of human society, and qualifies the situation
that they create with a radical criticism, briefer, less
profoundly theological, than Paul's, but just as radical: You
must all practise humility towards one another (5:5), the
older to the younger, and, perhaps harder still because the
old can be so stupid, the younger to the older.

To include the Johannine literature at this point in this
sketch of ministry in the New Testament may seem to step
out of the chronological line determined by Paul, 1 Peter, and
Acts. I am not arguing for an early date; the traditional
dating, which places the literature at the end of the first
century, seems to me to be correct, though the Apocalypse
probably incorporates earlier material. It is mainly a matter
of convenience. Johannine Christianity shows few of those
marks of development and systematization, whether in
organization or nomenclature, that we shall observe in the
fourth lecture, though it does show some signs of lateness and
reflects an increasing measure of institutionalization. At the
same time, along with other tendencies that we shall observe,
the literature contains not precisely the criticism, on theological and moral lines, that Paul had directed to a developing ministry, but a continuation of it. The constitution of the
Johannine community has been much discussed in recent
years; here we shall, as far as possible, consider it only under
the aspect of ministry.

Here there is no great quantity of evidence; and much of
what there is is enigmatic. It has often been held that the
liturgical assemblies described in the Johannine Apocalypse

as taking place in heaven should be regarded as based upon
what the writer had seen in the church on earth. In heaven
there is a composite heavenly figure (the Lamb in the midst of
the throne of God) surrounded by a group of twenty four
presbyteroi (Rev. 4:4; etc.); may we not see here a
transference of the bishop, or other chief minister, attended
by his elders—as depicted, for example, by Ignatius?
Unfortunately the picture is spoiled, as far as its earthly
counterpart is concerned, by the presence of four beasts, one
like a lion, one like an eagle, one like an ox, and one like a
man. Who are the beasts in the earthly sanctuary? Perhaps it
would be well not to try to answer that question; we must not
expect precise parallels between the earthly and heavenly
courts.

    We are on safer but not very productive ground if we turn
to the contents of the Seven Letters (Revelation 2, 3). In these
churches there are apostles (2:2); at least, we hear of bogus
apostles, but the fact that it seems worth while to lay a false
claim to be an apostle proves that there were also real ones,
and proves at the same time that the apostles in question were
not the Twelve Apostles of the Lamb, whom it would have
been easy to identify and to distinguish from the shams. It
seems natural to suppose that these secondary apostles cir-
culated among the churches; had they remained at one spot
their false credentials would have been immediately exposed.
Similarly the existence of Jezebel the false prophetess (2.20)
shows that the churches had real prophets; the category was
known, like that of apostle. It is probable that both apostles
and prophets were itinerant ministers. This would make it
easier for unscrupulous teachers to impose on communities
where they were not known. The pattern is thus similar to
that of the *Didache* (according to which apostles and
prophets appeared from time to time in the local communities, usually passing on but occasionally desiring to
settle and in that case subject to testing: *Did.* 11-13). Was this
the only ministry the churches of Revelation possessed? Was
there in addition a local, resident ministry, similar to that of
bishops and deacons in the *Didache* (*Did.* 15.1,2: Appoint for
yourselves bishops and deacons who are worthy of the Lord,
men who are meek, free from the love of money, faithful,

tested and approved, for they too carry out for you the ministry of prophets and teachers; so do not despise them...)? And who were the "angels" of the churches, to whom the seven letters were addressed? Do these stand for local ministers? It is hard to think of any sense in which John could believe that the letters he penned were directed to supernatural beings, and we recall that the word *angelos* is after all a common Greek word, bearing the meaning of *messenger*. Were the *angeloi* members of the churches to whom was committed the task of sending messages to other churches, and correspondingly of receiving messages from other churches? We are reminded of the Clement referred to by Hermas (*Vision* II 4.3). Hermas must send one copy of his vision to Clement, and Clement will send it to the foreign cities (*tas exō poleis*), for that is his job (*ekeinōi gar epitetraptai*)—to receive and transmit messages. This is an attractive suggestion; it is against it that elsewhere in Revelation angels, *angeloi*, are undoubtedly supernatural beings.

There is however support for the resultant picture, of an itinerant group or groups of wandering preachers, coupled with a leading figure who, no doubt with other duties, has laid upon him the task of communicating with other local churches, in the two shorter Johannine epistles. These are both written by a person who describes himself as *ho presbyteros*, the elder, one to a church (*eklektē kyria*, the elect lady), the other to an individual, Gaius, who may have been the equivalent figure in another church. The Second Epistle (2 John 7) tells us of many deceivers who have gone out into (*exēlthen eis*) the world; that is, they have at one time been members of the church. The Elder considers that they have left it for the world; that is, they have apostatized; but verse 10 suggests that they are visiting other churches, and may perhaps reach that to which the letter is addressed: If anyone comes to you and does not hear this doctrine with him, do not receive him into the house. This means that he would, if permitted, enter the house; that is, he would enter the fellowship of the house church; and if admitted, would teach the pernicious doctrine he has brought with him. Men of this kind, though it is clear that they still think of themselves as Christians, are to be cut clean out of the Christian fellowship. The Third Epistle shows that this was being done; unfortunately (from the writer's point of view) it was being done to his own envoys. Diotrephes, a man who loves to occupy the first place (*philoprōteuōn*), does not receive the Elder (the writer of the letter); not only does he not receive him, he circulates slanderous reports about him; not only does he reject the Elder, he refuses to "receive the brothers, and those who are willing to do so he forbids and casts out of the church" (3 John 9,10).

As far as form goes, we are in the same ecclesiastical world as in Revelation. The local church has a local leader; and among the churches there circulates a group of itinerant preachers and teachers. They are not uniformly and universally acceptable. The preachers approved by the Elder are not accepted by Diotrephes; equally there are those with whom the Elder is unwilling even to exchange a civil greeting. We recall the reference to those who say they are apostles, and are not (Rev. 2:2); the Nicolaitans, and those who approve their teaching and example (Rev. 2:6,15; cf. 2:14, "the teaching of Balaam"); there are also prophets—at least, there is a prophetess, whose teaching and morals are alike condemned (2:20,21). Here then are churches, we may say with some probability in the province of Asia, where there is a local and also a peripatetic ministry. We may perhaps go a little further, noting that it seems to be usual for presbyters to be found in plurality, and that Diotrephes is described as *ho philoprōteuōn*, the man who loves to have the first place. E. Käsemann (as others have done before him) thinks of Diotrephes as a bishop, one who exercises (or seeks to exercise) sole rule in his own church and also to maintain the doctrine and discipline in which he believes over a wider area. May we not say that *the* Elder, *ho presbyteros*, is in precisely the same position? Each behaves autocratically, expelling those of whom he disapproves; each extends his influence beyond his own community through his reaction to the peripatetic ministry. The Elder looked across the frontier and saw a figure he disliked; perhaps he was gazing into a looking-glass. Dr Käsemann indeed saw in Diotrephes a bishop who represented the *ecclesia catholica*, and in the Elder's church a sectarian group of enthusiasts. It is nearer the truth to say that both groups were similarly organized. It takes a strong measure of Christian humility to make monarchical episcopacy work.

The resulting picture is in truth not an edifying one, though as far as the structure of church and ministry goes it is surprisingly clear. It needed then, and the same situation always needs, a further Johannine contribution. I have deliberately begun with 2 and 3 John because if we were to begin with 1 John we should find, at first sight, little to help us. Having seen something of the pattern, however, where it is clear, we may trace it out again when it is further from the surface. The author of 1 John (and we must not assume that he wrote 2 and 3 John too) is able to address his readers as his "little children" and to remind them of the commandment they heard from the beginning. He writes with an authority more persuasive than that of the Elder because, though firm, it is less overbearing. He is an elder who is *presbyteros*, an older man. He has no need to lay claim to the title because he is confident that he will be accepted and his words heeded. There are however wandering preachers who are causing trouble. "They went out from us, but they did not belong to us" (1 John 2:19). They speak with the inspired utterance that carries conviction, and they have learned from the world how to speak in such a way that the world will listen (4:5). Since they evidently make the claim, "I know God" (e.g. 2:4) we shall not be far wrong if we call them gnostics. They have picked up the terminology, and with it some of the content, of current religious philosophy, and we need not question their good intention to use what they have learned in the interests of the Gospel. What, after all, is the use of preaching in a style to which no one will listen? The writer has two tests for them: not their learning or their popularity, but first, "Do they in their preaching point to Jesus as Christ and Son of God in the flesh?" and secondly, "Do they love?" Human love does not generate God; we love only because he first loved us and for that reason sent his Son in our flesh (4:10); but to deny, or refuse, love is to deny God. Ministry has but one function: to point, in a great variety of different contexts and in innumerable different ways, to Jesus Christ; and it works if, and only if, it operates in humility and love.

From this observation it is proper to turn to the Fourth Gospel, which originated in this world of warring ecclesiastical factions, of presbyters who wished to be first among their fellows, of wandering preachers who were ready to tickle their hearers' ears with the latest piece of philosophical speculation. Of all this the gospel shows us not a trace. It does indeed show how some of the language of gnosis can be used to bear witness to the Word become flesh, and it can deal out some hefty apostolic blows and knocks where the Jews are concerned. But of all the books of the New Testament it perhaps more than any other deals with its environment in terms of the paradox that I have several times stated in these lectures. One's first impression on reading through the gospel is that the ministry (in our sense of the word) is of no interest at all. Jesus does indeed call and appoint twelve disciples, but one of them is a devil, and at the last hour of his ministry Jesus tells the rest that they have not begun to understand him (16:31f.). In the end, indeed, they believe, but this does not set them above or apart from others. "It is because you have seen me that you have believed; blessed are they that have not seen me, yet have believed" (20:29). Yet again, that they have seen is their true significance; their importance is that they are witnesses, those who have seen and because they have seen declare what they have seen. They are not important as theologians or as administrators, but only as bearers of a word of testimony. Even this function they cannot carry out of themselves or on their own. "When the Paraclete, whom I will send to you from the Father, the Spirit of truth who proceeds from the Father, when he is come he will bear witness about me; and you too bear witness, because you have been with me from the beginning" (15:26,27). And the mark of their discipleship, the authentication of their testimony, is humility and love (13:15,16,20,35).

The writer of the supplementary chapter 21 brings out the two functions of ministry as he sets side by side the two outstanding followers of Jesus, Peter and the Beloved Disciple. Peter is to be the shepherd of Christ's flock—not his flock, but Christ's: "Feed my lambs, shepherd my sheep, feed my sheep" (21:15,16,17). The Beloved Disciple is the witness:

"This is the disciple who bears witness concerning these things and wrote these things, and we know that his witness is true" (21:24). Between them they manifest the dual qualification of all ministry: "Yes, Lord, you know that I love you": "the disciple whom Jesus loved." Loving and loved: how far the Presbyter and Bishop Diotrephes qualified is not for us to say. If the wandering preachers did not point to Jesus Christ come in the flesh, and did not love, they were not what John understood by ministers. Even apostles, as such, are neither here nor there; as bearers of the Word, as men created and shaped by love, they are at the heart of the Gospel.

If among the purposes he had in mind for his second volume Luke intended to include an account of the origin, authorization, and functions of the Christian ministry he was singularly unsuccessful in carrying out his intention. The apostles indeed appear; only twelve of them. Judas's place is filled by one who meets the double requirement—he is a witness of the resurrection and was a companion of Jesus throughout his public ministry (1:21,22); no one else, apparently not even Paul, qualifies for the title. All the Twelve are witnesses, but, in the narrative as we have it, only one speaks. Only once or twice (14:4,(14)) is Paul described as an apostle, nor is he described by any comparable term, though he is, at 13:1-3, one of the prophets and teachers at Antioch, but he stands out as the first of Christian preachers, and as a pastor who cares for the continuing life of his converts, ministering to them himself and also providing presbyters to take the lead in the churches in his absence (14:23). The apostles have the same theoretical base as in John; that is, they are witnesses to fact, and are empowered by the Holy Spirit for the purpose. Yet Luke is unprovided with stories, except about Peter, to represent them as fulfilling their mission.

Luke has little to tell about the origin and work of other ministers. He does not recount the origin of the order of deacons. It is true that in chapter 6 he recounts the appointment of Stephen and his six colleagues. But the word *diakonos* is not used, and to set out to describe the origin of the diaconate without using the word deacon is a scarcely credible undertaking. In the context (6:4) the apostles declare that they will devote themselves to the *diakonia* (service,

ministry) of the word, and this may be thought to imply
another *diakonia*, performed in a different way—in service to
the needy, such as widows. But the mere implication of the
nomen actionis can hardly serve as a substitute for the *nomen
agentis*. Of course it is true that when the order of deacons
did eventually develop the deacon's work was primarily this
diakonia rendered on behalf of the church to the poor. But
the setting of the narrative is Jewish, and in Judaism neither
the collectors of alms (*gebā'ēy ṣedāqâh*) nor the distributors
of alms (*meḥalleqēy ṣedāqâh*) were called by any word
suggestive of *diakonos*. On the other hand it is proper to note
that the seven who are appointed to deal with the distribution
of relief are established in their office by a formal procedure,
which however is described by Luke in a somewhat loose
way. The seven were chosen not by the apostles but by the
community as a whole. The community presented them to
the apostles. According to the Western Text (manuscripts D
and E) the apostles then prayed and laid their hands upon the
men whom the people had chosen, but the Old Uncial Text,
which is probably to be preferred, leaves it unclear who
prayed and laid hands on the seven—or rather, if the grammar
of the sentence (*estēsan . . . kai proseuxamenoi epethēkan*) is
taken strictly, says that those who presented also prayed and
imposed their hands. Did Luke mean this? Or did he think of
action by the apostles and express himself carelessly? It looks
as if the Western Editor wished to remove what he regarded
as a possible misinterpretation and to give the act of ordination unambiguously to the apostles.

We may, I think, draw the conclusion that Luke, who
undoubtedly attached great importance to the Twelve
Apostles, wished to indicate that they played an important
part in the institution of the Seven; he certainly wished to
assert full unity between the two groups, the Twelve and the
Seven. But he had no legalistic interest in setting down carefully the part that the Twelve played. He was not describing
the institution of a permanent order, though he probably
thought that the procedure he described would serve well on
other occasions when similar appointments had to be made:
let there be a popular choice, and let it be formally ratified by
the heads of the community.

The Seven soon disappear from the pages of Acts. We shall meet Philip and his work in Samaria and on the road to Gaza in the next lecture; and at 21:8 we find him settled with his daughters in Caesarea, and described as *ho euangelistēs*, the evangelist. We also however meet others who seem to occupy official positions. In the church of Antioch there were prophets and teachers who formed, apparently, a group distinct from the church as a whole (13:1-3). Among them were Barnabas and Saul, who as a result of an intervention by the Holy Spirit were separated for a special task. The work to which they were called is evidently that described in the following chapters: they were to be travelling evangelists. Their separation was marked by fasting and (as with the Seven) prayer and the imposition of hands. This act can hardly be thought of as ordination; the two men were in the group of prophets and teachers and, according to the narrative in Acts, had already for a long time been engaged in Christian work. The imposition of hands, like the prayer by which it was accompanied, sought God's blessing upon them in the new venture to which they were being commissioned. It may be that they were in this way made *apostoloi*, envoys, of the church of Antioch; they are described as *apostoloi* at Acts 14:4,(14) and nowhere else in Acts. This however is not the sense in which Luke used the word *apostolos* (though it may have been so used in his source. We see once more that Luke was aware that God chooses men to act as his servants and expresses his choice through human agents, but quite unconcerned about any ecclesiastical status they may have or the way in which they receive that status.

Teachers, *didaskaloi*, are not mentioned elsewhere in Acts. Christian prophets had previously been mentioned at 11:27 (a group of them came from Jerusalem to Antioch; one was called Agabus, who is mentioned again at 21:10); and at 15:32 we learn that Judas and Silas, who accompanied Paul to Antioch after the Council, were prophets. It is clear from 2:17,18 that Luke regarded prophecy as a gift of the Holy Spirit, but the other passages show that though the gift might be given to all there were some who were known to exercise it habitually. This however did not mean that it was ever exercised except as an immediate gift.

There remain in Acts the presbyters, or elders: 11:30; 14:23; 15:2,4,6,22,23; 16:4; 20:17; 21:18. In most of these passages it is simply assumed, without explanation, that they exist and that they are leading members of the churches. They receive charitable gifts, and, no doubt, are responsible for distributing them (11:30), so that some have seen in the Seven of Acts 6 not deacons but presbyters. There may be some support for this in that they appear in chapter 15 alongside the apostles, apparently the second rank among the church leaders. It is perhaps a special case of this when in 21:18 James, the only remaining member of the apostolic, or quasi-apostolic, group, appears accompanied by a group of presbyters. James here looks not unlike an Ignatian bishop, supported by the presbyters, but he is not described as a bishop because, as will shortly appear, to call him an *episkopos* would simply align his with the *presbyteroi*. According to 14:23 Paul and Barnabas appointed presbyters for every church founded on the first missionary journey. Terminologically this is in conflict with the fact that Paul never uses the word *presbyteros*. It would not however be far wide of the mark to say that what Luke means in his use of the word is that when Paul took leave of the churches in, say, Derbe, Lystra, Iconium, he said to his earliest and best trusted converts (cf. 1 Cor. 16:15), "Please keep an eye on things for me till I can return", and that such people were, in Luke's day and in the churches known to him, described as presbyters. They were also described by another term, as is proved by Acts 20:17 taken with 20:28. Paul summons to Miletus the *presbyteroi* of the church of Ephesus, and declares that Holy Spirit has appointed them *episkopoi*. The two terms were in equivalent use for the same persons. This is not in dispute, and it is scarcely open to doubt that in Luke's experience presbyters were bishops and bishops were presbyters. More important is the fact that Paul's speech in Acts 20 gives us a number of indications of the way in which Paul —or perhaps we should rather say Luke—understood the work of ministers. It was the Holy Spirit who appointed (*etheto*) them; not the churches, not Paul. It is a consequence of this that the speech makes no provision for the appointment of new ministers; the presbyters are not told that they must ordain successors, for the good reason that the Holy Spirit who appointed them can be trusted to produce more when more are needed. They are not appointed to a full-time, paid position. They would do well to follow Paul's example and work for their living, in order that, so far from receiving payment for their work, they may be in a position to give money away to those who are in need. The whole drift of the speech is away from a professional, subsidized ministry to an unpaid, part-time one. The presbyters are to shepherd God's flock. What this means in detail is not described. When they are committed to the word of grace (20:32, cf. 24) it is surely implied that they are also to proclaim it, declaring, as Paul had done, the whole counsel of God (verse 27, cf. 20). It is worth noting that no word is uttered about the conduct of sacraments.

I have left myself time at the end of this lecture for only the briefest of conclusions; and there remains a quantity of material to take into the fourth lecture. What we have seen is a community of men and women, convinced that Jesus is alive, convinced that they owe their relation to God to what Jesus has achieved through his death and resurrection and realized for them by the Holy Spirit. All are related to God in the same way; all are equally his servants. But they come under both religious and secular, social pressures, which force upon them the issue of leadership—spiritual gifts, age, social position, wealth. There is little or no attempt to deny that these exist, or to allege that they are of the devil—that would eliminate one wing of the paradox; but they are never allowed to run away with the church—that would eliminate the other. There is one test both of ecstasy and of behaviour: Does it testify, Jesus is Lord? And this testimony is borne not only in the language of prophecy and tongue but in obedience to the Lord's command of love.

CHAPTER THREE

Sacraments

I introduced the second lecture, on Ministry, with the careful defensive statement that the discussion of such a subject was only a matter of convenience and must not be taken to imply that what we call "the ministry" was to be regarded as equivalent to the church, essential to the church, or even the most important element in the church. Except in the sense that every Christian is a minister, a servant, of Christ in the church, the ministry could be dispensed with. The church would still exist, though indeed I believe it would be poorer, and in the New Testament we encounter people, of whom Paul will serve as the clearest of all examples, who are called by God to evangelize, and to act as leaders and pastors in the communities that are gathered by their preaching. Not only do we encounter such people; when the New Testament speaks of them it uses a number of recognizable words: apostle, prophet, teacher, bishop, presbyter, deacon, evangelist, and so on. To say this is not to say that the New Testament uses such words in the same sense in which they are ordinarily used today; often there are significant differences. But at least there is linguistic as well as substantial material for us to use.

In this lecture we take up another way in which the church may be supposed to become visible, and visible in a characteristic form. Many would say that the church is never more clearly the church than when it is enacting its faith in such rites as baptism and the Lord's Supper. There is however one important difference. As we have seen, the language of ministry is fairly plentiful in the New Testament. The word *sacrament* never occurs. I have drawn attention to this—sufficiently obvious but usually ignored—fact elsewhere (in a discussion of sacraments in John), and do not wish to repeat myself, but it seems to me that the matter is too important to pass by. *Sacrament*, of course, is a Latin word, and *sacramentum* does occur in the Latin New Testament, always as a rendering of the Greek *mystērion* (which in other passages is not translated but transliterated into Latin as *mysterium*). *Mystērion* in later (but quite considerably later) Greek Christian usage came to be the word denoting what we call sacraments. The earliest use in this sense noted by G.W.H. Lampe (in the *Lexicon of Patristic Greek*) is found in Eusebius in the fourth century. This is the more striking in that Christian authors were aware of the pagan use of the word for religious rites. As a word, however, meaning a rite, they appear to have reserved it for rites which they did not use and did not like—as when, for example, at 1 *Apology* 29.2 Justin vigorously denies that "promiscuous intercourse is one of our rites" (*estin hēmin mystērion hē aneden mixis*).

What I have just said (though suggested by Lampe's *Lexicon*) may not be quite correct. Two earlier passages must be mentioned. In Ignatius, *Trallians* 2.3, we read of those who are ministers of the mysteries of Jesus Christ (*tous diakonous ontas mystēriōn Iēsou Christou*). Ignatius adds that they are not ministers (*diakonoi*—which can have the sense of waiters) of foods and drinks but servants of the church of God (*ekklēsias theou hypēretai*). On this passage Lightfoot writes that "in a later writer *diakonous mystēriōn* would probably refer to their attendance on the priest when officiating at the eucharist. But such a restriction of *mystērion* would be an anachronism in Ignatius." This seems to beg the question, though not only would the view Lightfoot rejects make Ignatius the first Christian writer to use the word *mystērion* of the eucharist; it would leave him very widely separated from the second. Ignatius however probably does mean that the deacons were not only Christian social workers but ministers entrusted, in a general rather than a specifically sacramental way, with the Gospel, though we cannot be quite as certain of this as Lightfoot was.

The other passage in which *mystērion* may have a meaning related to a Christian rite is *Didache* 11.11, a passage so obscure that I hesitate to offer a translation of my own. J. Stevenson (*A New Eusebius*, London, 1957; p. 128) renders it, "Every approved true prophet, who enacts a wordly mystery of the church (*poiōn eis mystērion kosmikon ekklēsias*)". Some have seen here a ritual marriage actually enacted by a prophet to represent the union between Christ and the church; it is better to confess our ignorance, simply noting that though there may be a reference to some kind of symbolic action it is not the action of a sacrament, since it is done by the prophet alone, and he does not teach others to do what he does. In particular, there is no clear, or even obscure, reference to any otherwise known Christian action or rite.

This discussion borders on the irrelevant; the fact that we are concerned with is that the New Testament has no word for sacrament. It would be quite fallacious to deduce that because the New Testament lacked the word it was also without the thing that the word now signifies; a thing will often come into being before appropriate language for defining it is devised—it is the existence of the thing that prompts the development of language, and there is no question that New Testament Christians dipped people in water and from time met and took food and drink together. We cannot even say that the lack of the word *sacrament* meant that little stress had been laid upon these actions or small importance attributed to them. We can however say that thought about them had not developed very far. Suitable terminology is always needed before thought can develop, and it seems clear that the New Testament church had not evolved a specific category in which it could place its initiatory washings and its common meals. Christians in the middle and the second half of the first century—the New Testament writers—had inherited from earlier days certain features of the common life. They could not doubt that these were part of their inheritance, of the tradition they had received. But with them they received the question what they should do with these customs and how they should interpret them. There were no ready-made answers. Baptism and the Supper antedated sacramental terminology, and therefore antedated sacramental theology. This is not to say that sacramental theology, when it did develop, was wrong (though it goes without saying that sacramental theolog*ies*, which have a way of contradicting one another, cannot all be right); but we must recognize that we have before us two kinds of problem. There is the question when and how the pre-theological customs arose, and the question with what justice theological interpretations were attached to them.

There is indeed a more fundamental question still. The word sacrament does not occur in the New Testament. Does the New Testament contain in fact any sacraments? It is clear that the answer to this question will depend on the way in which this post-New Testament word is defined. It will be well however not to anticipate anything on these lines. Sacraments have been, and are, defined not only theologically but liturgically, not only in words but in actions, and it is these actions, with water in baptism and with bread and wine in the eucharist, that provide us with the starting-point from which we ourselves proceed to formulate in our own minds the meaning of what takes place. This means, as we look back into the past, that we must first consider what the New Testament Christians did, and then discover, if we can, how they made theological sense of what they did. We must not start with pre-conceived, post-New Testament, ideas of what a sacrament is. We may reach some kind of definition before we finish.

If we are to do this we must separate the two chief actions, baptism and eucharist, and look at them separately—and I had better add that I shall not consider "those five commonly called sacraments", not because I am beginning from an arbitrarily chosen party position (though I do not see how Luther's *Babylonian Captivity* can be refuted), but because there is so little relevant material in the New Testament and other early Christian literature. I shall not follow the order of study that I used in the second lecture; it will, I think, be possible to set out the material more clearly in a different way.

This time I propose to begin with Acts, which purports to tell the story from the beginning, and in fact carries it on not merely to the time when Paul reached Rome but to the time when the book was written—much nearer, I believe, to the end of the century. It was inevitable that it should reflect the circumstances with which its author was familiar.

We may begin with baptism. It would be possible to select certain passages and deduce from them that Christian baptism was a waterless affair, a purely spiritual experience. "John on the one hand (*men*) baptized with water, but you on the other hand (*de*) shall be baptized in Holy Spirit" (Acts 1:5). One might conclude that the two baptisms, thus expressed in contrasting clauses, were completely different; the one a dipping in the water of the River Jordan, the other a receiving of the Holy Spirit as the power of a new life. There is some support for this not only in the narrative of the Day of Pentecost (which says much of the Spirit and nothing of water) but also in Peter's words at the end of his address: Repent, and let each of you be baptized for the forgiveness of your sins, and you shall receive the gift of the Holy Spirit (2:38). Acts 11:15,16, referring back to 1:5, could convey the same suggestion. "As I began to speak the Holy Spirit fell upon them (Cornelius and his companions) just as upon us at the beginning (on the day of Pentecost?). And I remembered the Lord's word, John on the one hand baptized with water, but you on the other hand shall be baptized with the Holy Spirit." The gift of the Spirit, made spontaneously to Cornelius, was baptism in the Holy Spirit; water was not involved. This passage, however, in fact shows that this was not Luke's understanding of the matter, for in the narrative (which I have quoted above as reported in chapter 11), Peter says, "Can anyone forbid the water that these men should not be baptized, men who have received the Holy Spirit just as we did?" (10:47). It would have been a more accurate way of expressing his thought if Luke had written, There are two baptisms, John's, which was with water only, and the new Christian baptism, which is with water and Spirit (cf. John 3:5). Another equally clear passage is Acts 8:36, where the Ethiopian says to Philip, "Look, here is some water. What is preventing me from being baptized?" For Luke, Christian baptism was a rite involving the use of water, but normally accompanied by the gift of the Spirit and effecting entry into the people of God. It was connected both negatively and positively with John's baptism: negatively in that it brought about what John's baptism may have pointed to but did not itself effect—the gift of the Spirit and entry into the redeemed community; positively, in that it was a continuation of John's rite and in that the things it did effect were things towards which John's baptism pointed. This is shown by the references to John in Acts, and also by the very significant place accorded to John in the gospel tradition.

You will however note the word *normally*. It has often been pointed out that, in Acts, baptism appears as a rule to be regarded as the means by which the Holy Spirit is given, but that there are exceptions to the rule. On the one hand, Cornelius and his companions receive the Spirit before baptism; Peter makes haste that the rite may catch up with the fact (10:44-8). On the other hand, Philip baptizes the Samaritans, including Simon the Magus, but they do not receive the Spirit until Peter and John lay their hands on them (8:12,13,15-17). I have argued elsewhere[1] that the point of this is not that only apostles are able to confer the Spirit or that confirmation is needed as a supplement to baptism. Luke is concerned rather to show that the Spirit is not subject to human control, whether by financial means (as in Simon's attempt to buy the right to confer the Spirit) or by liturgical means—it is possible to carry out baptism correctly and sufficiently (Philip's baptism of the eunuch required no supplement) but without the bestowal of the Spirit. I do not find it difficult to believe that this represents both Luke's view of the matter, and the facts themselves. If the Spirit is not Lord (*kyrion*) the Nicene creed is in error.

There is a second respect in which *normally*—and not universally—applies. Baptism appears very patchily in Acts. On the day of Pentecost Peter calls for it (2:38), and in response those who accept his message are baptized (2:41).

---

1 In my article "Light on the Holy Spirit from Simon Magus (Acts 8.4-25)" in *Les Actes des Apôtres*, ed. J. Kremer, Leuven University Press, Gembloux, 1979; pp.281-95.

He does not require it in the mission speech in chapter 3, and we do not hear of baptism again until in chapter 8 we reach the Philip stories, which we have just considered. Paul is baptized (9:18; cf. 22:16, but not the conversion story in chapter 26); Cornelius is baptized. In the whole of the "First Missionary Journey" (Acts 13,14) there is no reference to baptism. Christian congregations are established over a wide area and are (according to 14:23) provided with presbyters, but there is no record of any baptism; indeed we hear no more of baptism till Acts 16, when two households, those of Lydia and of the Philippian gaoler, are baptized. A number of baptisms therefore in Philippi, but still none is recorded in the old mission field of the First Journey. Silence again follows, for Amphipolis, Apollonia, Thessalonica, Beroea', and Athens, until we reach Corinth, where many of the Corinthians believed and were baptized (18:8). After this the only passage that remains is 18:24-19:7, where we learn the odd fact that Apollos, who knew only the baptism of John, was not baptized, and that the group of about twelve disciples in Ephesus, who knew only the baptism of John, were baptized, after which Paul laid his hands upon them. We must not make too much of these facts. We could not expect Luke to mention explicitly the baptism of every convert; but some of the gaps are large enough to be significant. It is as good as certain that Luke thought that baptism was a normal first step for a convert, but there were considerable parts of his source material that showed no interest in baptism. If Acts were our only source of information we could not legitimately infer that all Christian converts in the first century were baptized; the silence of some of the sources makes it seem very improbable that all were baptized.

References in Acts to the eucharist are even patchier than those to baptism; it is indeed uncertain whether there are any such references. The Christians are occasionally said to have a common meal, but it is always referred to as the breaking of bread. At Acts 2:42 they continue in *tēi klasei tou artou*, in the breaking of the loaf; at 2:46 they break bread at home (or possibly at their meeting-house, in contrast with the Temple). It was for this purpose that the Christians at Troas met (20:7,11). Their meeting, at least when Paul visited them, was a long one, and it included a sermon. We are not told that it, or any other of the meetings referred to, included the drinking of wine. Partly for this reason (but he had others), H. Lietzmann believed that there were two early forms of Christian supper. The first was a continuation of the meals that Jesus had been in the habit of taking with his disciples throughout his ministry. They still met as they had done in the past, and he, though now invisibly, was still present with them as they gathered in his name. This was an ordinary poor man's meal, and the main article on the table was bread. Wine, a relatively expensive commodity, was not used, or if occasionally it was served it was not essential to the meal. The second kind of Christian supper, perhaps initiated by Paul (but we shall be thinking about Paul's contribution later), looked back not to the general run of common meals shared by Jesus with his disciples but to the special meal which they shared on the last evening of his life, in the shadow of his death. This was symbolically represented by the use of wine, which stood for his shed blood. The remembrance of the blood "shed for you" led to the development of the simple "This is my body" into "This is my body which is for you" and "This is my body which is given, or broken, for you". At this point we remind ourselves that Acts has nothing to say about the use of wine; its words are "the breaking of bread". It is true that this phrase may have been used to suggest a whole meal, beginning with the breaking of a loaf but including other features also, such as the drinking of wine. This however is not explicitly mentioned; and a further problem is raised when we observe that, in addition to the passages I have already cited, Acts 27 also, in the account of the sea voyage, introduces the breaking of bread. Paul exhorted all, crew and passengers, to take some food. "And when he had said these things he took a loaf and gave thanks (*labōn arton eucharistēsen*) to God in the presence of them all, and when he had broken (*klasas*) it he began to eat. And they all cheered up and themselves partook of food" (27:35,36). Does this mean that the Christian meal (note the "eucharistic" language) was open to all? that the sailors were invited to share it with Paul and his Christian companions?

It is tempting to follow up this reference to wine, or rather

Luke's lack of reference to wine, though to do so may take us
a little off the main line of development of this lecture. I have
not yet raised the question of the relation of what we call the
eucharist to the narratives of the Last Supper as we have
them in the gospels. We cannot however forget the curious
material to be found in Luke's gospel—the first volume to
which Acts corresponds as the second. In the gospel in its
most familiar form we read

> 22:17 He took (*dexamenos*) a cup, gave thanks (*euchar-
> istēsas*), and said, Take this . . .
> 19 He took (*labōn*) a loaf, gave thanks (*eucharistēsas*),
> and broke (*eklasen*) it . . . saying, This is . . .
> 20 Similarly (*hōsautōs*) the cup after they had had
> supper, saying, This cup is . . .

Here we have two cups of wine (contrast Acts!) with a loaf of
bread between them. If we follow the Western Text and omit
verses 19b,20 we are left with the order, wine, bread—which,
I will note in advance, is to be found also in 1 Corinthians 10
and *Didache* 9. It suffices at the moment to observe that there
is evidence for a good deal of variety in the way in which
Christians observed their common meal.

So far we have confined our attention to Acts, which we
must take as good evidence for church practice at the time
Luke wrote. Whether the information it provides counts also
as good evidence for the period the book purports to describe
is another question, but in this case the odds are that it does,
for it is unlikely that a formal liturgical rite would develop
into an informal supper party, dignified by no more than a
religious atmosphere. There is in Acts little formality in
regard to either baptism or eucharist. It is only when we read
Acts in the light of the Third Gospel that we can use the latter
term. What we see in Acts itself is a simple unreflecting practice followed habitually by unreflecting Christian people. It
was natural to baptize newcomers to the faith, for had not
John the Baptist baptized genuine born Israelites as if they
had been Gentiles accepting proselyte baptism? If he had
been in this way preparing a people for the coming of the
Lord (Luke 1:17) the task was now more urgent than ever, for
the coming of the Lord was nearer, and the Lord had himself
begun the task of gathering the renewed people of God. The

association of baptism with the gift of the Spirit was in part pragmatic—the early church was an inspired, "pneumatic" community—and in part an early fruit of the theological evaluation of the unexpected interval between the resurrection and the parousia. And what could be more natural than that the new fellowship, cemented from within by a common loyalty to Jesus and from without by the pressure of resistance to this common faith, should meet from time to time in the unity of a common table? It is surprising, when other material that we shall shortly consider is borne in mind, that Luke should reflect such artless and unsophisticated conditions. Perhaps this should be set down to his credit as a historian; more probably it should remind us of the important fact that Christian theology, Christian practice, and Christian liturgy developed at different speeds and on different lines in different places. Luke's own church and its practice may not have been as developed as others had been a generation earlier.

It is not easy to know whether the material we have found in Acts is properly described as sacramental. It provides us, however, with a suitable base from which we can observe important developments which chronologically were a good deal earlier than the date at which Acts was written.

The chronologically earliest material we have about the way in which baptism and the eucharist were understood is to be found in 1 Corinthians 10. This is earlier than what Paul gives us of his own views in the next chapter in that Paul, in both chapters, writes in reaction to a state of affairs and a corresponding body of belief that he found in existence at Corinth; this is of course not to say that he formed an opinion of his own only at this time. The implication of 1 Corinthians 10 is clear. Paul recalls the story of Israel in the wilderness. They had a baptism provided by God himself, for they were baptized into Moses, in the cloud and in the sea (10:2). They had spiritual food and drink, for they ate the manna and drank from the rock (10:3,4). Yet, notwithstanding such privileges, they fell into gross sin, and having done so were drastically punished. These things happened, says Paul, as an awful warning for us (10:6). It is natural, and correct, to infer that the Corinthians were falling into the error of supposing

that because they had a baptism and enjoyed spiritual food
and drink they were secure against sin, and (if they sinned)
against punishment, and that they drew the conclusion (for
which there is confirmation in the rest of the epistle) that they
enjoyed complete ethical freedom and might behave as they
pleased. Their sacraments (but how glad we should be to
know what word they used to describe them!) gave them
complete protection, and thus were in effect a screen behind
which anything became possible.

So much is clear. Can we go further and find out what (in
the mind of the Corinthians) constituted baptism and the
supper as such a screen? It is, I think, fair to begin (though
not to finish) with the observation that Paul himself may
have to bear some of the responsibility. He had taught Christian freedom. "All things are lawful for me" was a proposition
with which he could not disagree, whether or not he had
himself formulated it. We must however go further than this.
There are in 1 Corinthians a few hints that we may pick up.

In regard to baptism: at the beginning of the letter Paul
recalls that members of Chloe's household had told him of the
incipient divisions in the Corinthian church. "Each of you has
his own watchword: I am of Paul, I am of Apollos, I am of
Cephas, I am of Christ" (1:12). In dealing with this repre-
hensible situation Paul immediately goes on to say not only,
"Was Paul crucified for you?" but also, "Were you baptized
into the name of Paul?" In this context he rejoices that he had
baptized very few of the Corinthians, and minimizes the
importance of baptism in comparison with preaching the
Gospel. He is fearful lest the Corinthians should think that,
because he had carried out baptisms, he had baptized people
into his own name. It is a reasonable inference that there were
in Corinth those who conceived that they had been baptized
into Paul's name, Apollos's name, Cephas's name, while
some rightly understood that they had been baptized into the
name of Christ (though they may have understood wrongly
what they stated correctly). This means that they understood
themselves to stand in a special relation to and under the protection of their own chosen leader. They said: It is not I, but
Paul, or Apollos, or Cephas, who must answer for my
actions; I am free. If they said, Christ will answer for me,

they were right; but to place oneself under Christ's protection is at the same time to place oneself under his direction.

Again there are pointers that may help to explain the Corinthians' attitude to the supper. First is the simple fact that the Corinthians must have found in their environment and in their pre-Christian experience of religion analogies to the new Christian meal as they understood it. These were for the most part meals that had behind them, or included in them, sacrificial rites—rites which (generalizing broadly) had the effect of placating a deity by a non-moral action. Coupled with this is the fact that the eating of sacrificial food was a notorious problem at Corinth, which Paul was obliged to discuss at length. Some at least of the Corinthians thought it legitimate not only to eat meat that had been sacrificed to idols (in this Paul agreed with them) but also to take part in rites carried out in an idolatrous shrine. It would thus be natural that the Corinthians should think of the new meal in an analogous way. This is confirmed by a second observation. Immediately after the passage (10:1-13) in which Paul warns his readers not to regard baptism and supper as conferring some kind of moral immunity, he goes on to speak of the supper not actually as a sacrifice but in relation to sacrificial meals. One might paraphrase 10:18-21 as follows: If you are going to speak of the supper as a sacrifice you had better have another look at empirical Israel. They have sacrifices, and those who eat them participate together in what the altar means. Heathen sacrifices mean participation in demons, and this is inconsistent with the Christian meal. You must choose between the Lord's cup and the demons' cup, between the Lord's table and the demons' table.

If it be true (and it seems hardly open to doubt) that local Corinthian thought about the Christian supper was exposed to influences of this kind, the result will have been a tendency to think that the quasi-sacrificial meal made things all right with the Deity; after the meal one was free to do what one liked.

One further observation may be made at this stage. It is hard to read Paul's account of the supper as practised at Corinth in 1 Corinthians 11 without drawing the conclusion that he is writing about a real meal, that is, one at which food and drink were used in such a way as to satisfy physical hunger and thirst. It may have had a symbolical element too, but it was not purely symbolic. Had it been working rightly the poor would have benefited when the wealthier shared their supplies with them. Paul gives no indication that he wished to change this arrangement, though naturally he disapproved of its perversion in which the poor went hungry while others got drunk.

As far as baptism is concerned Paul's reaction is clear, and I have already indicated it. I cannot understand 1 Cor. 1:14-17 as implying anything less than a relative depreciation of baptism. Doubtless all, or most, of the Corinthian Christians had been baptized (though 1 Cor. 15:29 may imply that a number had died without baptism), but Paul had paid little attention to the matter, and now was glad of his disregard for it. No one should say that he had tried to collect the Corinthian Christians into a Pauline party, baptized into loyalty to him.

The story of the supper is more complicated, and there are two points which it is important to make. The first of these is Paul's insistence on the importance of the context within which eating and drinking take place. This derives from his treatment of the question whether it is or is not permitted to eat food that has been sacrificed to idols. This question is complicated by the consideration that the Christian must always be motivated by love and by respect for his brother's conscience. The consequence of this is that he will sometimes abstain from doing things which he would otherwise be free to do; in the interests of clarity I shall leave out this consideration, important as it is. Paul distinguishes two cases: one is the private eating of food bought in the *macellum*, or market, after ritual, sacrificial slaughter. There is no harm in this; the Christian need make no inquiries; he may eat it freely. He must however at all costs flee from idolatry, and may not take part in a pagan sacrificial rite, or a meal included in such a rite. The cultic, idolatrous setting gives a new significance to the eating. That is, the idolatrous significance of eating does not lie in the substance of the food eaten but in the context in which the food is eaten. This is so closely bound up (in 1 Corinthians 10) with what Paul says about the Christian cultic meal that it seems reasonable to draw the conclusion that for him it is not the substance of the bread and wine consumed that is important but the context of Christian fellowship, of life under the authority of the Lord, that is significant and gives significance to the meal itself and to the bread and wine.

That this should be so makes all the more terrible and destructive the denial of Christian fellowship and of the Lord's authority that was all too manifest at Corinth. Paul's horrified reaction is clear, and it leads to the second point that is to be made here. He cannot praise the Corinthians for their behaviour (1 Cor. 11:22). What is to be done? It is at this point that Paul gives a traditional account of the Last Supper, or at least of certain central acts and words in it. Now it is almost universally assumed that, then as at the present day, these so-called "Words of Institution" and the corresponding acts, played a central part in every celebration of the supper, and that Paul was saying to the Corinthians, "Mend your ways by recalling that solemn moment from which your church supper originated, in the night in which the Lord was betrayed. Your present practice is a contradiction not merely of Christian principle but of that very meal which you profess to continue, or repeat it." It must however be acknowledged that Paul does not actually say this. What he does is to compare their meal with one in which the Lord took part; and he speaks about proclaiming the Lord's death. If this means that the supper (when well conducted) included a narration of the passion, this may well have included, as the synoptic passion narratives do, an account of the farewell meal; but this is another matter. It is true also that Paul's traditional account of the supper contains the words, "Do this in memory of me" (11:24), and, "Do this, whenever you drink, in memory of me" (11:25). We shall consider these words later; one possible meaning they may bear is that Christians should remember the Lord at every meal. And verse 27 gives the impression of a fresh argument used by Paul against the Corinthians: If, as I have now told you, bread is to be interpreted as the body, wine as the blood of the Lord, you must take care to eat and drink worthily.

There is a strong case for supposing that it was Paul who

associated the Last Supper with the Lord's Supper, with the
Christian fellowship meal in which all believers pledged their
loyalty to the Lord, who, they believed, was truly though
invisibly present. Paul did this to remove scandals from the
supper; also, no doubt, to give it a new, higher significance.
If this was so, one familiar problem is immediately solved.
The question has often been asked why an annual meal, the
Passover, celebrated on a particular occasion by Jesus and his
disciples, became a weekly, or even daily, event. The answer
may well be that there was no problem. In the first instance
the church's supper was not connected with the Last Supper
and the Passover but was a weekly celebration of the Lord's
resurrection day, in which the Lord's coming was invoked, or
perhaps simply a fellowship meal held as often as was convenient. It would be entirely like Paul that he should not only
call the church to order but set its acts and celebrations in the
light of the cross. We may perhaps see another hint of this in
1 Corinthians 5; we must cleanse the church, Paul says, from
incest and any such defilement because we are like Jews
observing the Passover who must rid their household of the
"old and wicked leaven".

Here we may look back to what Paul has done with baptism. The verb (*baptizein*) occurs ten times in 1 Corinthians,
but we have already had all but one of these occurrences (in
1:13,14,15,16,17; 10:2; 15:29 (twice)) before us. The remaining
one is at 12:13: In one Spirit we were all baptized into one
body, whether Jews or Greeks, whether slaves or free. This is
given a special Pauline turn and plays a part in Paul's
development of the image of the church as Christ's body, but
it is essentially the central Christian notion which we have
seen in Acts: baptism is a rite of initiation, and the church,
the group into which the candidate is being initiated, being
what it is, it is connected with the Spirit. We need not linger
here. Elsewhere the word occurs but seldom, and we must
not follow those who seem incapable of seeing an aorist tense
without suspecting an allusion to baptism. By far the most
important passage is Romans 6. I quote 6:3,4: "Do you not
know that we who were baptized into Christ Jesus were
baptized into his death? So we were buried with him through
baptism into death, in order that as Christ was raised from

the dead through the glory of the Father so we also might walk in newness of life." Paul has done here with baptism what we have seen that he did with the supper. He has taken a rite used previously in the simple sense of entry into and participation in the Christian fellowship and attached it explicitly to the death and resurrection of Jesus. I say that he has "taken and attached"; should I have said that he found this attachment to the death and resurrection of Jesus already in existence, and approved of it? Much (but not everything) will depend on the way in which the opening word of 6.3 is taken: *agnoeite*, Do you not know? Paul uses this and similar expressions when referring to themes that his readers should have been familiar with, though he fears that they may have forgotten them. "Do you not know?" has the sense, "Surely you do know and cannot have forgotten altogether." Had Paul then ground for thinking that the Roman Christians, before he had visited them and taught them, were already familiar with the connection between baptism and the crucifixion and resurrection? If so, we must draw the conclusion that he was not himself responsible for this connection. It may be so, and it is perhaps not of great importance that we should be able to name the first man to perceive this truth. We must however remember that Paul cannot have known much about the Roman church, and may have been making an unjustified assumption, taking it for granted that they would be familiar with the doctrines that he taught in churches of his own foundation. He was certainly the most influential, and possibly the first, Christian to insist upon the connection between baptism and the death of Christ.

We need not here attempt to answer the question whether Colossians is a Pauline or a Deuteropauline work; in Col. 2:12, as in Romans, baptism is associated with the death and resurrection of Jesus. In Gal. 3:26,27, baptism is connected with another very characteristically Pauline phrase, *en Christōi*: Through faith you are all sons of God in Christ Jesus; for all of you who were baptized into Christ put on Christ.

Paul found himself obliged to deal with a situation in which both baptism and the church supper were getting out of hand. They were out of hand religiously, in that people

supposed they worked *ex opere operato*, guaranteeing to
those who participated in them complete security against sin
and the consequences of sin. Baptism admitted them to a
community in which all things were lawful, and where incest,
for example, became a source of pride (1 Cor. 5:2: You have
come to be puffed up, *pephysiōmenoi este*); and the supper
maintained their place in that community. The same rites
were out of hand socially, in that those who were baptized
attached themselves to those who had baptized them, as if
these were party-leaders rather than servants of Christ, and
added to the divisions in the church by turning the fellowship
meal into an occasion of rioting for the wealthy and hunger
and shame for the poor. In this situation Paul used the only
corrective that he knew; he proclaimed Christ crucified, and
insisted that the Christian rites should bear witness to the
Christian faith, and that they became effective only in the
context of obedient faith which looked to but one *kyrios*, the
Lord who was crucified. In the case of the supper he secured
this end by anchoring the church's meal to the Last Supper, in
which (so old tradition told him) the Lord himself had connected bread with his body and wine with his blood.

I turn now to look at the Synoptic Gospels, all of them
written later than the latest Pauline letter. I shall not allow
myself in this lecture to discuss the events of the Last Supper
from the historical point of view. I believe that the supper
was a Passover, and that Jesus used the framework and some
details of the Passover rite to explain some of the significance
of his work, but I shall not attempt to justify this opinion.

The Marcan account of the Last Supper already reflects not
only a situation within the life of Jesus but also the post-
pauline situation, in which the Last Supper had come to be
determinative of the church's liturgical action. When we move
from Mark to Matthew it seems clear that what we observe is
the tidying up of what was taken to be a liturgical text.
"Take, this is my body" becomes more explicitly "Take, eat;
this is my body". "They all drank of it [a historical state-
ment]; and he said, This is my covenant blood" becomes
"Drink ye all of it; for this is my covenant blood". To "shed
for many" is added the interpretation "for the remission of
sins". The church had learnt the Pauline lesson and was

expressing it in liturgical terms; in its common assembly it must do and say what Jesus did and said on that notable occasion when, in the shadow of the cross, he celebrated Passover with his disciples.

Luke takes a step further, and it is at this point that I propose to linger for a little while. It is in Luke (and in 1 Corinthians 11) that we meet the commandment, Do this (*touto poieite*) in memory of me (*eis tēn emēn anamnēsin*). Both the origin and the meaning of the command have been much disputed. If it was indeed spoken by Jesus on the eve of his crucifixion it is best understood as the same kind of paradox that he spoke with reference to the woman who anointed him. "She has anointed my body for burial; this is the only anointing my body will receive, for when later you look for it it will not be there—there will be no corpse for you to anoint:" So here: "If you are going to hold a memorial feast for me you must do it now; the future will be no time for memorials of one who is vindicated and alive." The present imperative, *poieite*, was doubtless taken by those who read the gospels in Greek to have iterative force—Do repeatedly, again and again; but Hebrew and Aramaic do not distinguish present and aorist imperatives, so that if Jesus himself used these words, his imperative, "Do this", would relate simply to the present, like the other imperatives, "Take and eat", "Take and drink."

This brings us back to the difficult and textually confused Lucan narrative, which I have already referred to. It is impossible here to discuss the textual evidence in full; it is more complicated than the simple omission of 22:19b and 20 by some Western manuscripts. This and other variations probably arose because the full text of verse 16-20 seemed to be at variance with the customary practice of taking first the bread and then the wine. The confused state of the long text, which I believe to be original, is, I think, best explained on the view that Luke combined two sources; both of them took the conventional order, eating then drinking, but one of them was primarily a historical source, relating, or purporting to relate, a historical event in the life of Jesus, whereas the other was a liturgical source, in which the historical event was refracted through later Christian practice. The first source is in verses 15,16,17,18:

> I have greatly desired to eat this Passover with you
> before I suffer, for I tell you that I will not eat it again
> until it is fulfilled in the kingdom of God.
> And he took a cup and gave thanks and said: Take this
> and divide it among yourselves; for I tell you that
> henceforth I will not drink of the fruit of the vine until
> the kingdom of God comes.

Here are two parallel sayings, one relating to eating, the other
to drinking, and both carrying tremendous eschatological
emphasis (which is present, though not quite so emphatically,
in the Marcan narrative also). They give a complete account
of the Last Supper, understood in its historical context. The
liturgical source is contained in verses 19,20.

> He took a loaf, gave thanks, broke it, and gave it to
> them, saying: This is my body which is given for you;
> do this (that is, Go on doing this) as my memorial.
> And similarly he took the cup, after they had had
> supper, saying: This cup is the new covenant in my
> blood, which is being poured out for you.

I am aware that what I have said is hypothetical, and can
be no more than hypothetical. Apart from the use of Mark by
Matthew and Luke all source criticism of the gospels is a
matter of hypothesis. It is however more than hypothesis that
behind the narratives of the Last Supper there stand both
historical and liturgical interests; and it is precisely this
combination, rather than any particular disentangling of
combined sources, that concerns us for it shows that Paul's
attempt to control the church's fellowship meal by means of
the Last Supper succeeded, at least in the churches represented by Matthew, Mark, and Luke, and these between
them probably covered a good deal of ground.

It is therefore with great surprise that we turn to the Fourth
Gospel. This is a matter that I have discussed elsewhere[2] and
must therefore handle briefly now. It will however provide us
with a convenient summing up of this lecture.

Take baptism first. As in the other gospels we hear a good

2 In my Commentary on St John's Gospel, 2nd ed., London, S.P.C.K.,
   1978, pp.82-5; and in *Essays on John*, London, S.P.C.K., 1982, pp.80-97.

deal about the baptizing work of John—the Baptist. In 3:22,23 Jesus is said to be baptizing at the same time as John, and at 3:26 the message is brought to John that Jesus is being more successful than he—"Just as it should be", says John. At 4:1 the Pharisees hear the same report, and Jesus hears that they have heard it; only, the evangelist adds, it was not Jesus himself who was baptizing, but his disciples. All this makes up a curious, rather twisted, account; it is difficult to deduce much from it. And this, if we are thinking of occurrences of *baptisma, baptizein*, is all. There is no command to baptize comparable with that of Matt. 28:19. But there are allusions. There are few who would deny some sort of allusion in John 3:5: "Unless one is born of water and Spirit he cannot enter into the kingdom of God", though many think that the words *hydatos kai*, "*water and*", have been inserted by an editor into a text that did not originally contain them. In 13:1-17 Jesus washes the feet of his disciples; when Peter objects to this, Jesus replies, "If I do not wash you, you have no part with me." That is, the washing is an act indispensably necessary if one is to live a Christian life in communion with Christ. Here too an allusion to baptism is often thought to be probable. Finally, in 20:23 Jesus commissions and authorizes his disciples: "If you forgive anyone's sins they are forgiven, if you retain them they are retained." Here we seem to be very near a command to baptize *eis aphesin hamartiōn*, "for the forgiveness of sins"; but it is significant that even here, as in John 3 and 13, there is no explicit mention of the rite. Those things which elsewhere in the New Testament are brought into connection with baptism—the Spirit, cleansing, rebirth, forgiveness—are all present, but are left, and were, we may suppose, intended to be left without the focal point which might unite them and give them liturgical coherence.

Consider the supper. The farewell meal of Jesus with his disciples is narrated at great length, but it is not a Passover meal, and no reference is made to the eating and drinking of bread and wine or to any words connected with them. We cannot say that John had no interest in Paschal themes; he represents Jesus as the true Paschal lamb who died at the very time that the animal sacrifices were being slaughtered in the Temple, fulfilling all that they foreshadowed. Nor can we say (though some would contradict me here) that John was not interested in, or even wished to depreciate, the Christian supper. I do not look upon John 6:51-58 as an interpolation by an ecclesiastical redactor, not least because it seems to me that to treat the passage as a piece of quasi-magical sacramentarianism is exegetically mistaken. In fact John offers a critique of such exaggerated and unguarded sacramental theology as appeared a few years later in the epistles of Ignatius (who writes of the eucharist as a medicine conferring immortality, an antidote against death; *Ephesians* 20.2) and no doubt was already current when John wrote. That he was unaware of the Christian practice of meeting, perhaps weekly, for supper is highly improbable; that he wished to bring this practice to an end hardly less so. That he was critical of what his contemporaries were making of a practice in itself innocent and indeed desirable is, on the other hand, probable—Paul had been similarly critical in the preceding generation. But whereas Paul wrote 1 Corinthians at a time when men were cutting the Christian meal loose from its origin in Christ and turning it into a pagan cult or a secular orgy, so that the necessary correction was to anchor the meal in a concrete moment in which the self-giving of Jesus on the cross was crystallized in his body and blood, represented by the bread and wine, John wrote at a time when the Christian rite was in danger of becoming a mechanical repetition of the Last Supper, which was believed to secure, *ex opere operato*, eternal life for the recipient. Thus John, first, focused Paschal significance not on a meal but on Jesus crucified himself—*he* was the Lamb of God in his own action; secondly, detached what he had to say about eating the flesh and drinking the blood of the Son of man from the Last Supper; and, thirdly, embedded these references to eating and drinking in a discourse which made it clear that receiving Christ, the bread of life, by faith belonged to a wider setting than a cult act, even though the cult act (which is clearly in mind in John 6) might be a particularly clear focusing of this receiving. The Last Supper narrative was thus left clear for an acted parable of the humble love of Jesus for his own, a parable that represents the historical fact of his death, which is at once the means by which he unites men to himself (13:8; 12:32), and

the pattern of love to which they must conform their lives
(13:14,34,35).

In this, as in many other respects, the Paul-John axis is
determinative in New Testament theology. This is not
intended to depreciate other parts of the New Testament,
which give us many beautiful and powerful variations on the
theme which it would have been good, if time permitted, to
explore; but the theme itself is stated by Paul and John. And
it makes as clear as anyone could hope that sacraments (I
return to this problematical word, which the New Testament
does not use, and hope shortly to give it some sort of definition) display with special clarity that paradox of centrality
and peripherality which I have said is characteristic of the
church, its members and its actions, in the New Testament.
There is a true sense in which baptism and eucharist are those
parts of Christian practice which the church shares with
every other society. You have to get your name on the books
somehow; and it is very natural for a group of people, united
by a common interest and concern, to mark at least some of
their meetings by a common meal. We can, I believe, see
some of the ordinariness of this in various parts of the New
Testament (notably Acts), and can see elsewhere some of the
perversions to which it inevitably became subject in a
heathen environment; we have evidence not only for Corinth
but also (in the Apocalypse of John) for the churches of Asia,
and some of the allegations brought against Christians and
rebutted by the Apologists may have been founded in fact. It
seems to me quite probable that groups existed, describing
themselves as Christian, where for example it was customary
to end the supper party by putting out the lights and prac-
tising a very unchristian kind of freedom. How was the poor
pagan to know which were the real Christians and which
bogus? One may feel some sympathy for him. It was the
work of Paul and John (and it is important that, doing that
work in different historical contexts they did it in different
ways) so to hold baptism and supper to the central Christian
fact of Christ crucified and risen that the two actions became
central manifestations of the essential pattern of Christian
existence.

It is important that they should be both peripheral and

central, important that they should be ordinary actions. In the technical language of medieval theology the *matter* of baptism is water, the *form* the words, including the name of the Trinity, accompanying the water; the *matter* of the eucharist is bread and wine, the *form* the words of institution. But in fact the matter of baptism is not only water; it is the fact that baptism, carried out in the New Testament way by immersion, looks like any kind of secular initiation— including even the horseplay of schools and army camps. The matter of the eucharist is not merely bread and wine, but the Rugby Club's annual dinner. And the great achievement of the New Testament church, under its leaders Paul and John, is that by attaching the matter to the form, 'which is the word, the word of the cross, the offer of the Spirit, the promise of forgiveness, it made both actions a standing witness to the truth of its own being. In this way we may begin at length to approach a New Testament definition of a sacrament; for if there are sacraments in the New Testament, this is what they are. Unlike the Word, which has its own kind of objectivity, such a sacrament must always hover on the brink of the banal or the perverse; but in the believing community it is a testimony to Jesus, who now ever lives as the crucified one, because it is a place where the transformed ordinariness of creation, which is the stuff of Christian existence, becomes strikingly visible, and in the Word the promises are heard.

CHAPTER FOUR

The Developing Community

"Gather up the fragments that remain, that nothing be lost."
The words came unbidden to my mind as I looked back over
the first three lectures and began to write the fourth. The
difficulty is that they are not fragments that remain but very
large pieces; and there are more than twelve basketfuls of
them. Before however we begin to collect some of them it will
be well briefly to retrace our steps and observe the ground
that we have covered.

The stiffest hurdle to overcome was the first: How do we
effect the transition from Jesus of Nazareth, the Palestinian
Jew, to the post-resurrection, and eventually mainly Gentile,
church? The key lies in the eschatological interpretation of
history, even though this eschatological interpretation
demanded reinterpretation almost before it had itself been
fully grasped. God, it appeared, meant to vindicate his
obedient Son not immediately and to all the world but in
two stages, denoted respectively by resurrection and
parousia. The church was the community of the interim; and
in the early years it must have found its understanding of
itself changing at a great rate. The proportional difference
between year 2 and year $(2+1)$ is very different from the proportional difference between year 2000 and year $(2000+1)$,
and the paradox of a body that is simultaneously central and

peripheral appears differently as time elapses; the balance alters but the rate of change diminishes with the passage of the years. Since the church by definition exists between two moments in time it is necessarily a visible thing—at least, part of it will always be visible, and to observe it in its visibility we considered ministry and sacraments, choosing them not as the most important but as the most crassly visible elements in the church's life. It might have been better, though it would have been very much more difficult (perhaps through lack of evidence impossible), to trace the church's understanding of ethics and its achievement in that field. These two topics, ministry and sacraments, which have of course received only the sketchiest treatment, provided their own versions of the paradox of the central and the peripheral. But both gave the church more than new kinds of paradox for theologians to play with. They gave it some of the necessary apparatus of permanence—a practical commodity needed by a society that was to go on existing for a long time, though once more a paradox, for this long-living church needed not so much guarantees of its permanence as reminders of its essential temporariness, which it was always too ready to forget; for it was—and never can be anything but—a company of pilgrims, on the march between the present age and the age to come. The church had and has an impossible task, for it can affirm itself only at the cost of denying its own proper being.

In this fourth lecture our main endeavour, in addition to a general tidying up, will be to consider what the church made of this impossible task. We could describe the task in another way by saying that we have to look at that phenomenon which goes under the name of *Frühkatholizismus* (literally, early catholicism). I use the German word because I do not at this stage wish to commit myself to an English equivalent; and this may serve as a useful caution, for *Frühkatholizismus* is evaluated differently by different people. If it is regarded as a bad thing, the late first and second century church, which produced it, may offer the excuse that it can hardly be blamed for failing to perform adequately what we have described as an impossible task. If *Frühkatholizismus* is regarded as a good thing, it can nevertheless, in its actual form, or forms, never be judged a wholly good thing, because the task the church was performing when *Frühkatholizismus* was evolved was an impossible one, and impossibilities are seldom achieved. Indeed the time when things go wrong arises when the church comes to believe that it has achieved the impossible, that it has succeeded in affirming itself without destroying itself. But this is enough of generalization; the sooner we get down to some plain history and exegesis the better. Let us first look again at some parts of the New Testament that we have already considered.

It has often been claimed that Acts shows many of the features of *Frühkatholizismus*, but examination of the text shows that this is, in most respects, a mistaken view. It is simply not true that Acts sets out the beginning of a story and a theory of ministerial succession from the apostles. The Twelve have a hand in the appointment of the Seven; but the Seven then virtually disappear. One is soon killed; five leave the stage and are heard of no more (unless Nicolaus becomes the father of heresy; see Rev. 2:6,15); one, Philip, reappears in Acts 8 and 21, but all he has done towards perpetuating the ministry is to have four daughters who prophesied, and since they were virgins that line of succession is unlikely to have gone any further. The Twelve had no hand in the appointment and commissioning of Paul; indeed, it was hard to persuade them that he was a genuine Christian and not an *agent provocateur*. Paul is not represented as forming the first link in a chain connecting the apostles with the later ministry. At 14:23 it is said that Paul and Barnabas appointed presbyters in every church (of the First Journey), but when in Acts 20 Paul addresses the Ephesian presbyters he does not say that he had appointed them, and gives them no instruction about appointing others. This speech (as I have said) sums up Luke's view of ministers: the Holy Spirit can be trusted to provide them as required.

We have also looked at baptism and the supper in Acts. The most interesting fact here is that there is so little tension between early sources and late redaction. Luke himself has no rigid code of practice in regard to baptism, and his understanding of the common meal is simple in the extreme. I see no trace of any kind of development or sophistication at all, still

less any of a kind that could be labelled *Frühkatholizismus*.
The breaking of bread at sea provides a good example (27:35).

The very fact that Luke writes a history means that his
church has come to terms with history; that is, it has
recognised that since God evidently intends history to go on
there must be some meaning in it. Eschatology remains, but
not as the determinative factor in the church's life. It can
hardly be said that theology is developed and formalized;
there are fewer traces of formulation in Acts than in the
Pauline epistles. There are signs of anti-gnostic interest,
especially in Paul's insistence that he has made public
proclamation of the whole content of Christian truth,
keeping nothing back (20:20,27), but there is no attempt to
answer gnostic doctrine in its own terms. Simon is not, as in
later literature, represented as a gnostic, but simply as—a
magus; his crime is not false doctrine but simply—simony.
The exalted position of the Twelve and of other notable
figures is a mark of natural respect and of Luke's anecdotal,
biographical style of historical writing. The Twelve and
others are reported to have worked miracles; so were many
others in antiquity. Acts is, in my opinion, a late first century
work; but it is not *frühkatholisch*, in any sense that can
reasonably be applied to that term.

We have also spent a little time on the Johannine literature,
and may briefly recapitulate. If we may assume that the five
Johannine books came not all from one hand but from one
area they reveal a situation marked by a good deal of variety,
and probably of development. The epistles show, so far as I
can see, no interest in either baptism or the Lord's Supper.
There may be an allusion to the baptism of Jesus in 1 John
5:6, but if there is it is relatively devalued in that it requires
the cross to be taken with it: He came "not with the water
only, but with the water and the blood". In Revelation the
eucharist may be in mind in 3:20: "Behold, I am standing at
the door and knocking; if anyone hears my voice and opens
the door, I will come in to him, and I will have supper with
him and he with me." But there is little to build on here; the
verse might be no more than a vivid image of a personal relation between Christ and the believer; it is perhaps significant
that though it may no doubt bear a general reference to the

church it is cast in the singular number *(tis)*; it would have been easy to use a plural or collective. The evangelist takes his own line, critical, I think, of contemporary use of the sacraments. I shall say no more about his attitude to the supper; as to baptism, so far from his having added, as many think, at 3:5, the words *hydatos kai* (of water and), it seems more likely that, if editing took place, he added *kai pneumatos* (and of Spirit); certainly, if we may judge from the rest of the paragraph, the element that interested him, and could not be omitted was Spirit, not water. What I mean is that, as in his treatment of eucharistic material he emphasises the role of the Spirit and writes in such a way as to discourage a growing *ex opere operato* view of the eucharist, so in his allusion to baptism he may be countering a belief that dipping in water was in itself, apart from the personal work of the Spirit, a sufficient means of regeneration. If a *frühkatholisch* view of the sacraments means one that tends toward the mechanical, even indeed the magical, it may perhaps be seen in the background of the Johannine literature (though this is to some extent a matter of—probable—conjecture); it is not to be seen in the literature itself.

It will be remembered that E. Käsemann takes the view that the Johannine literature emerged from a sectarian group of spiritual enthusiasts, who stood over against a catholic church led by Bishop Diotrephes. This view seems to me to be at variance with the evidence of the epistles. That the Johannine group contained "spiritual" persons, prophets, who uttered oracles for which divine authority was claimed, is undoubtedly true; but it also felt itself threatened by such persons, and the author of 1 John found it necessary to give his readers the warning, "Do not believe every spirit, but test the spirits to see whether they come from God, for many false prophets have gone out into the world" (1 John 4:1). The phenomena of inspiration are not in themselves a guarantee of authenticity, and the test to be applied is not a question of the degree, measure, or mode of ecstasy, but of orthodox belief: "This is how you know the Spirit of God: every spirit that confesses that Jesus Christ has come in the flesh is of God, and every spirit that does not confess Jesus is not of God" (4:2,3). Passages such as 1 John 3:24 ("This is how we

know that he abides in us, from the Spirit which he gave us")
must be read in the light of this test. Coupled with the test of
orthodoxy is the test of love: "Let us love one another, for
love is of God, and everyone who loves has been begotten of
God and knows God. He who does not love has not come to
know God, for God is love" (4:7,8). It is unnecessary to show
that for John love, if real, must be a matter not of speech but
of action. Those who had gone out from the church into the
world claimed to know God; we may not unreasonably call
them gnostics. Their claim was, according to the writer of 1
John, falsified by their lack of love and by the very fact of their
having left the body which he, John, represented. "They went
out from us, but they did not belong to us, for if they had
belonged to us they would have stayed with us" (1 John 2:19).

No criticism is implied of what may, so far, have been well
justified action on the part of the writer of the epistle; but his
attitude is that of an organized, institutional church rather
than that of an enthusiastic group. It is (as we have seen)
further hardened in 2 and 3 John, in the mutual excommunication of the Presbyter and Diotrephes. If we are to call
Diotrephes a bishop, the Presbyter was (to adapt Milton) a
bishop writ differently, for he, it seems, was as ready as his
rival to rule by excommunication. The church has now
become a territory with clearly drawn boundary lines, based
upon dogma and discipline. Similar lines appear, drawn, one
may say, in different colours, in Revelation. The Fourth
Gospel is different, both profounder and more liberal in its
theology. The apostles have an important place, but it is
based upon their hearing and keeping the word of Jesus.

It has taken us a long time in these lectures to reach the
Pastoral Epistles (which I take to have been written in the
generation after Paul in the attempt at once to defend him
against those who questioned his authority and to say what
he would have said had he still been present[1]), although these
might have seemed the right place at which to begin a
discussion of Church and Ministry in the New Testament—of
church and ministry, but not of sacraments, for though the

1 For a different view see e.g. J.N.D. Kelly, *The Pastoral Epistles*,
London, A. & C. Black, 1963, especially pp.30-34.

recipients are given many instructions on how to behave in church, how to conduct their ministry, these instructions include nothing on the conduct of baptism and eucharist. There is indeed only one reference to a sacrament, at Titus 3:5, where "the laver (*or* washing) of regeneration and renewal by the Holy Spirit" appears to be a reference to baptism. This is a striking fact.

The church itself is, in the Pastorals, taken for granted as a going concern. It looks back to the epiphany of our Saviour Jesus Christ who emptied death of its power and brought to light life and immortality (2 Tim. 1:10) when he came into the world to save sinners (1 Tim. 1:15), and forward to final judgement and reward, the crown of righteousness which the Lord, the righteous judge, will render "to me on that day", "and not to me only but also to all those who have loved his epiphany" (2 Tim. 4:8). At 1 Tim. 3:15 the church is described as the "pillar and bulwark of the truth" (that is, of the Gospel), a description that has often been misunderstood. It does not mean that the Gospel exists only by the courtesy, and through the support, of the church; rather that the church exists in order to serve the Gospel, supporting and defending it by making it known. Christians are defined (2 Tim. 2:10) as the *eklektoi*, the elect, those whom God has chosen, with no reference to any virtue of their own (Titus 3:5). At 2 Tim. 2:19 this is reinforced by the Old Testament quotation, The Lord knows those who belong to him" (Num. 16:5). Thus the church is grounded in and lives by the Gospel of God's electing grace. This is perhaps not said quite as often or as plainly as in the genuine letters, but it is certainly said.

In 2 Tim. 2:19 there is a second Old Testament quotation: "Let every one who names the name of the Lord depart from unrighteousness" (Num. 16:26; cf. Isa. 52:11; 26:13). Those who invoke the Lord must see to it that their lives conform to his requirements; that is, the church, though consisting of saved sinners (1 Tim. 1:15), who are justified by mere grace independently of any works that they have done (Titus 3:7,5), must exercise discipline to see that its members should make it their business to practise virtue (Titus 3:8).

Grace and discipline are thus key words for the understanding of the church in the Pastorals. This appears notably

in the ethical teaching of the epistles. There is more explicit
commandment and detailed advice than in the genuine
Pauline letters, with less attempt to relate specific instructions
to a theological basis. This was inevitable and necessary; life
is too short, and our brains are too poor, for us to think out
every moral decision from first principles. It means however
that Christian life was being lived at a lower theological
tension. In the new historical-eschatological situation
(though it is not really new—these epistles still stand
"between the times", though the two decisive moments seem
further apart) this was inevitable, and it is less than fair to
dismiss the epistles as "bourgeois ethics"—though in any case
it is reasonable to ask why "bourgeois" should be regarded as
an opprobrious term. The fact is that the Christian is now
expecting to live for some time as a member of the "bourg".
Ethical teaching is not, and is not regarded as, "natural", but is
rooted in God's command (1 Tim. 1:5), and is sanctioned by
his reward (2 Tim. 4:8). Quiet content is a characteristic
virtue (1 Tim. 6:7,10), but this is by no means asceticism.
Asceticism was practised by the adversaries, who appear to
have been gnostics of a sort, and it is condemned because it is
contrary to the Christian (biblical) doctrine of creation. It is
wrong to forbid marriage, and various kinds of food and
drink (1 Tim. 4:3; 5:23; 6:17).

An important motive is the reputation of the church with
the outside world—not that the world's judgement is in itself
valid, but in that a bad reputation can endanger the effect of
the Gospel: 1 Tim. 3:7; 6:1; Titus 2:5; 3:8,14. It is of a piece
with this that the virtues enjoined are those that the non-
Christian world in general recognized—for example 1 Tim.
3:1-7; Titus 2:4. Ministers, who will be particularly exposed
to the world's scrutiny, must be especially careful in this
respect.

This is the angle from which to approach the teaching of
the Pastorals about ministers, who have too often been
viewed simply in terms of the occurrence in these letters of
the undoubtedly interesting and important, and frequently
disputed, words *episkopos, presbyteros, diakonos*. I have
said that grace and discipline are the key words for the
understanding of the church in the Pastorals; they are also the

key words for the understanding of the ministry. The fundamental functions of the ministry are to preach the Gospel of
the grace of God, and to maintain discipline. These functions
are often represented in mixed, even jumbled, exhortations,
for example in 2 Tim. 4:1-5: "Proclaim the word, keep at it in
season, out of season, reprove, rebuke, exhort . . . Be sober
in all things, suffer hardship, do the work of an evangelist,
carry out your ministry to the full." As more precise
examples we may note the minister's responsibility for
guarding the deposit (*parathēkē*) of sound doctrine (1 Tim.
6:20; 2 Tim. 1:12,14), and his duty of resisting error (1 Tim.
1:3; 2 Tim. 2:25; Titus 1:13; 3:10f.). He must be an example
to the flock: "Be an example for the believers in speech, in
behaviour, in love, in faithfulness, in purity" (1 Tim. 4:12).

The "technical" ministerial terms are indeed important, but
they are not yet fully technical. In 1 Tim. 3:8-13 *diakonoi* are
undoubtedly a special class of ministers. We learn in this
paragraph something of their necessary moral qualifications,
nothing of their duties. We cannot be certain whether 3:11
refers to female deacons or to the wives of deacons. It is
however also to be noted that if Timothy behaves well he will
be a good *diakonos* (1 Tim. 4:6) and that he and Paul both
have a *diakonia* (1 Tim. 1:12; 2 Tim. 4:5). We can hardly
think of these two as belonging to the lowest order of clergy;
in these passages the words must be general; minister,
ministry; that is, servant, service.

According to J. Jeremias, at 1 Tim. 4:14 the "laying on of
hands of presbytery" (*epithesis tōn cheirōn tou presbyteriou*)
is equivalent to the Hebrew *sᵉmîkat zᵉqēnîm*, and the verse
means that Timothy has been ordained to the presbyterate.
This is easier to believe than that he was a deacon, but in the
epistle as a whole the meaning of *presbyteros* has evidently
not become settled. At 1 Tim. 5:1 the *presbyteros* appears
along with *neōteroi, presbyterai,* and *neōterai* (younger men,
older women, younger women); he can hardly be anything
other than an "older man", who as such must be treated with
respect. A similar group appears at Titus 2:2f., with
presbytēs, the word that occurs at Philemon 9 (Paul the
aged), in place of *presbyteros*. Returning to 1 Timothy 5 we
find that the word *presbyteros* appears to be moving in a

"technical" direction; at 5:17 we read that the *presbyteroi* who preside well are to be counted worthy of *diplē timē*, which means *double honour* and may also, as some think, imply *double pay*. If this view is right it means that ministers are now being paid, and on a graduated scale. This would make an interesting contrast with Acts 20 (see above, pp.52f.). important however is the interpretation of *"presbyteroi* who preside well". There is evidently a contrast here. Is it between Those who preside well, and Those who preside badly? or between Those who preside (and do it well), and Those who do not preside? Or is it possible that all three groups—Those who do not preside, Those who preside, Those who preside well—are in mind? The second half of the verse (Especially those who work at preaching and teaching) must mean that not all *presbyteroi* preach and teach; some, we may infer, are simply *presbyteroi*, that is, older men with no special gift for leadership. As in 1 Peter 5 (see above, pp.41f.), we are presumably at a stage where the age differential and the leadership differential were not fully and clearly distinguished. It is worth while to note 1 Tim. 3:6: it was unwise to appoint new converts to ministerial functions.

Titus 1.5-7 suggests very strongly that the words *presbyteros* and *episkopos* describe the same persons, though no doubt from different—sociological and theological—angles. This is confirmed by the absence of *presbyteros* from 1 Timothy 3, which goes into some detail about bishops and deacons. We may turn back to 1 Tim. 5.17: Were those presbyters who singled themselves out as good preachers and teachers described as *episkopoi*, though they also remained *presbyteroi*? One can only guess.

Timothy, whom we may take to be intended to be a representative minister, was ordained to his work: 1 Tim. 4:14;2 Tim. 1:6; compare also 1 Tim. 1:18. He was pointed out by the Spirit (either because he himself spoke in the Spirit or because other inspired persons designated him), and through prayer, accompanied by the laying on of hands, a *charisma* was given him to do his work. Charismatic and institutional appointment are now combined; a very important step.

We must note one other feature of the Pastorals before we leave them. Whereas in other epistles we follow form-critical methods in order to detect traditional pieces of teaching, woven by the author into his own work, the author of the Pastorals deliberately points out such things, calling attention to them as "faithful sayings" (1 Tim. 1:15; 3:1; 4:9f.; 2 Tim. 2:11-13; Titus 3:8). See also 1 Tim. 3:16. It is sometimes doubtful whether the saying follows or precedes the formula; and there is textual uncertainty at 1 Tim. 3:1. With a good deal of fudging it is possible to get out of these passages something like a creed.

We believe in
1. *The living God, the Saviour*
2. *Jesus Christ, who came into the world to save sinners*
3. *who died and rose from the dead*
4. *The Holy Spirit, who has been poured forth*
5. *Baptism for regeneration*
6. *The hope of eternal life.*

It would be more than rash to argue that such a creed ever existed. The greatest interest of these faithful sayings is not their content but the fact that they existed. The formalizing of a ministry was accompanied by the formalizing of doctrine into brief memorable statements. It may be, however, that A.T. Hanson is right in thinking that *pistos ho logos*, "faithful is the saying", is the author's own formula, designed to draw attention to statements he considered to be of special importance.

Finally we must take a quick summarizing look at the Pastorals and the picture of church, ministry, and sacraments that they provide. On the whole (but with some exceptions) it is a surprisingly primitive picture. Not only is the church aware of living between the two comings of Christ, its existence determined by this strange eschatological situation; it believes that it is living in the last days: that is why there are those who pervert the Gospel and threaten to destroy the church. There is no reference to the Lord's Supper. Is this because the writer, or writers, thought it a matter of relatively slight importance? or because it was now a matter of secrecy, which could be disclosed only to the initiated and was therefore not to be set down on paper? I do not see in the epistles any hint at concealment. As in John but not Paul, baptism is referred to in terms of regeneration; but the agent of regeneration and renewal is the Holy Spirit, not water; again, we are reminded of John. Terminology for the ministry is developing. There are still older members who gravitate to the top of the structure of respect, if not of power, so that younger men, even if outstandingly able, are apt to be looked down on: "Let no one despise your youth" (1 Tim. 4:12). It was however becoming clear that not all old men were born leaders; perhaps it was only the ablest *presbyteroi* who came to be called *episkopoi*. There was a separate group of *diakonoi*, but whether they were assigned to eleemosynary duties or acted more generally as assistants we do not know. We do know that the ministers were repeatedly charged to preach and teach, and to keep gnosticism at bay. One verse (2 Tim. 2:2) takes thought for the future: Timothy must commit the things he has heard from Paul to trustworthy men, who will be able in turn to teach others; that is, a succession of teachers is envisaged, teachers who can be trusted to maintained the deposit (in this verse note *parathou*, "commit", which is related to *parathēkē*, "deposit") of truth that originated with Paul.

There remain a few parts of the New Testament at which we have not even glanced, but it is time to pause in order to survey and assess the position we have reached. In the later New Testament books the church has recognised that it is a historical phenomenon, that it is an entity with a history. It started some time ago and has persisted through a number of decades; the degeneration of the present time may suggest that the end is not far away, but it would not do to depend on this—Christian truth must be safeguarded for the next generation, and for the generation beyond that, even if these are the "last times". There are deadly perversions of Christian truth; if gnosticism means a docetic denial of the human fleshly reality of Jesus Christ it sets itself outside the Christian pale and is totally unacceptable. Christians must learn both to say their prayers and to take an appropriate place in society. They must come to some kind of terms with the Roman state, and they must learn that though their roots are in the Old Testament they are not Jews; the Jews have rejected *their* Messiah and thereby disfranchised themselves from the people of God.

All these things were in fact true, and the church is not to be blamed for recognizing truth. It had an even longer history ahead of it than any, I think, of the New Testament writers clearly saw. The question was not whether it should recognize this situation but how it should deal with it. Would it do so in such a way that its own integrity was preserved, or would it clutch at the wrong kind of security and so (but for the grace of God) destroy itself? It must be said frankly that even in the New Testament there are places where one trembles for the ark: defensive measures in Acts, where Paul appears to placate Rome by arguing that Christianity is only a somewhat improved version of Judaism; passages in the Johannine epistles, where the writer seems to identify truth with his own formulation of it and to excommunicate those who do not accept his formula; again, passages in the Pastorals which show an unpauline unwillingness to argue and prefer to retreat into safe formulas. I have exaggerated and caricatured; brevity demands it. Whether one can describe what I have drawn attention to as *Frühkatholizismus* already apparent in the New Testament depends on how *Frühkatholizismus* is defined; let me say (with an eye to what I shall say later) that we may see perhaps some of the ingredients of *Frühkatholizismus*; and that there is a difference between a collection of ingredients and the finished product.

This is the point at which we may step outside the New Testament and take up the story at and just after the stage at which (with a few exceptions, such as 2 Peter) the latest books in the New Testament were written—Acts and John, perhaps in the 90s. The First Epistle of Clement probably belongs to this period. It is a long work, and we cannot hope to survey the whole of it. It is in chapters 40-44 that the form of the church is dealt with, and most of the topics we have considered find at least allusive reference there.

The whole passage, indeed the whole epistle, is about order. The Corinthians are a disorderly crowd. Clement has read 1 Corinthians and he knows what they were like in Paul's time.[2] "Take up the epistle of the blessed Paul the Apostle. What wrote he first to you in the beginning of the Gospel? Of a truth he charged you in the Spirit concerning himself and Cephas and Apollos, because that even then you

had made parties" (47:1-3). Now they are at it again; and
this will not do. "Let each of you, brethren, in his own order
give thanks unto God, maintaining a good conscience, and not
transgressing the appointed rule of his service, but acting
with all seemliness" (41.1). The Old Testament shows God's
desire for good order, and things are not different under the
new covenant.

Order is to be preserved by a well ordered and orderly
ministry. Again, the pattern is provided in the Old Testament.
"Unto the high priest his proper services have been assigned,
and to the priests their proper office is appointed, and upon
the levites their proper ministrations are laid. The layman is
bound by the layman's ordinances" (40.5). The reference to
high priest, priest, and levite suggests a threefold order of
ministry, and the epistle does indeed mention *episkopoi,
presbyteroi,* and *diakonoi;* but it must not be assumed that
these denote three orders. We have seen passages in the New
Testament where the two terms *episkopos* and *presbyteros*
are applied to the same persons; according to Lightfoot,
Clement also identified them. In 42.4,5 we read only of
bishops and deacons, and in 44.4,5 Clement writes: "It will be
no light sin for us, if we thrust out those who have offered the
gifts of the bishop's office (*ta dōra tēs episkopēs*)
unblameably and holily. Blessed are those presbyters who
have gone before . . .". Perhaps the evidence justifies a
compromise solution, and we should rank Clement with 1
Timothy and guess that both documents come from a time
when the group of presbyter-bishops was beginning to split
so as to produce two distinct orders.

These ministries were originated by the apostles. 'The
Apostles received the Gospel for us from the Lord Jesus
Christ; Jesus Christ was sent forth from God. So then Christ
is from God, and the Apostles are from Christ. Both therefore

Footnote from p.89

2. I have used Lightfoot's translations of Clement and Ignatius mainly in
   order to avoid any appearance of bias in the treatment of controversial
   passages. It need not be said that Lightfoot's renderings are excellent
   though from time to time different views are possible, and some passages,
   notably (among those quoted) 1 Clement 44 and Ignatius, *Ephesians*
   5:2, would merit long and detailed discussion, if space permitted.

came of the will of God in the appointed order. Having therefore received a charge, and having been fully assured through
the resurrection of our Lord Jesus Christ and confirmed in the
word of God with full assurance of the Holy Ghost, they
went forth with the glad tidings that the kingdom of God
should come. So preaching everywhere in country and town,
they appointed their first fruits, when they had proved them
by the Spirit, to be bishops and deacons unto them that
should believe" (42.1-4). This, Clement adds, was no hastily
thought-up scheme; it fulfilled the Old Testament, and he
quotes, or rather misquotes, Isa. 60:17, introducing *diakonoi*
where they are not to be found, and transforming *episkopoi*
from task-masters into bishops. The apostolic message was of
the coming of the kingdom of God (*mellein erchesthai*), but
Clement cannot have thought that the apostles believed that
it was going to come soon, for according to him, not only in
chapter 42 but even more explicitly in chapter 44, they took
great care to secure a continuous supply of ministers. "Our
Apostles knew through our Lord Jesus Christ that there
would be strife over the name of the bishop's office (*epi tou
onomatos tēs episkopēs*). For this cause therefore, having
received complete foreknowledge, they appointed the afore-
said persons, and afterwards they provided a continuance
(*metaxu epimonēn dedōkasin*), that if these should fall asleep
(*ean koimēthōsin*), other approved men should succeed to
their ministration (*diadexōntai heteroi dedokimasmenoi
andres tēn leitourgian autōn*). Those therefore who were
appointed by them (*hyp' ekeinōn*), or afterward by other
men of repute (*metaxu hyph'heterōn ellogimōn andrōn*) with
the consent of the whole Church, and have ministered (*leit-
ourgēsantas*) unblameably to the flock of Christ in lowliness
of mind, peacefully and with all modesty, and for long time
have borne a good report with all—these men we consider to
be unjustly thrown out from their ministration (*tēs leitourgias*)"
(44.1-3). I may here add explicitly (see p.90) that I have used
Lightfoot's text and rendering of this notoriously difficult
passage, not because I think it beyond criticism but because it
does at least afford a solid basis for further discussion.

What Clement says finds little support in earlier Christian
literature—that is, in the New Testament. We may point to 1

Cor. 16:15, where the household of Stephanas are said to be
the firstfruits of Achaea. Paul however does not say that he
appointed them as bishops or deacons, but that they appointed themselves *eis diakonian tois hagiois*, for ministry to the
saints. We have noted the probability that early converts
would tend to assume positions of leadership; Clement had
read 1 Corinthians and probably developed the verse about
Stephanas in terms of what he knew of the ministry in his
own day. How much of his picture is due to this kind of
development? Probably, so far as the evidence allows us to
judge, a good deal. But the evidence is descriptive rather than
prescriptive. If in Rome or Corinth you were looking for
leaders you would be foolish if you did not first consider men
(and, remembering Phoebe, women) whom Paul had, if not
appointed in a formal sense, approved of; and as time went
on, you would look to those whom these approved (*ellogimoi*)
men had chosen and themselves approved. We see this hap-
pening (though in relation to teaching) in the Pastorals:
"The things you have heard from me through many witnesses
commit to trustworthy men, who will be able to teach others
too" (2 Tim. 2:2). But what of the Pauline fellowship, where
everyone had a psalm, a teaching, a revelation, a tongue, an
interpretation (1 Cor. 14:26)? of the Pauline church, in which
every member had its function or ministry, like the organs
and limbs of a body (1 Cor. 12:4-27)? This, it seems, has
disappeared. Perhaps not at Corinth; perhaps that was in
part the cause of the trouble—Clement's trouble, that is.

The Pastorals are concerned that ministers of the generation
of Timothy and Titus should pass on the doctrine they
learned from Paul to others who in turn may teach a third
generation; and so on. Teaching and preaching are, as we
have seen, the main, almost the only, activities of ministers in
the Pastorals. It is not so in 1 Clement. What does Clement
expect to be done by the church's ministers? "The offerings
and ministrations (*tas te prosphoras kai leitourgias*) He
[Christ] commanded to be performed with care, and not to be
done rashly or in disorder, but at fixed times and seasons
(*hōrismenois kairois kai hōrais*) ... They therefore that make
their offerings at the appointed seasons (*hoi oun tois
prostetagmenois kairois poiountes tas prosphoras*) are

acceptable and blessed: for while they follow the institutions
of the Master they cannot go wrong" (40.2-4). "It will be no
light sin for us, if we thrust out those who have offered the
gifts of the bishop's office unblameably and holily" (44.4). I
have not quoted Old Testament passages cited by Clement,
but there can be no doubt that they helped to formulate his
understanding of the Christian ministry as a priesthood
whose duty was to make offerings to God. The presbyters, or
bishops, "led the prayers and thanksgivings of the
congregation, they presented the alms and contributions to
God and asked His blessing on them in the name of the whole
body. Hence Clement is careful to insist (40) that these
offerings should be made at the right time and in the right
place and through the right persons" (J. B. Lightfoot, *The
Apostolic Fathers*, Part I. *S. Clement of Rome*, Vol. II, p.
135). If the Lord did lay down institutions concerning the
times, seasons, and places at which appropriate liturgical
actions should take place, and about those who should carry
out such actions, none of the evangelists saw fit to record
them. This, not in itself but in the sort of concern that it
shows, is not unimportant. But the most serious question at
issue here is (not a particular interpretation of the substance
of the eucharistic elements but) the direction (if one may put
it so) in which they move. Even when he comes nearest to
using sacrificial language, in 1 Corinthians 10, Paul thinks of
the bread and wine as gifts from God to men, not from men
to God: "The cup of blessing which we bless, is it not a
sharing (*koinōnia*) in the blood of Christ? The loaf which we
break, is it not a sharing in the body of Christ? . . . Consider
Israel after the flesh; Are not those who eat the sacrifices
partakers (*koinōnoi*) of the altar? . . . You cannot drink the
cup of the Lord and the cup of demons; you cannot partake
of the table of the Lord and the table of demons" (10:16-21).
For Paul, the eucharist is a receiving, a joint partaking of, a
divine gift to men. The Lord offers a cup, and so do the
demons; the question is which men will receive. To say this is
not to say that for Paul there is no sacrificial element in the
Christian life. There is; but sacrifice is offered in the common
stuff of daily existence, and the priest who offers it is at the
same time the sacrifice that he offers: I beseech you,

therefore, brothers, by the mercies of God, to present your
bodies, a living sacrifice, holy, acceptable to God, which is
the true worship you should offer (Rom. 12:1). The rest of
the chapter explains how the offering is made.

Rather less than a couple of decades more will take us to
Ignatius, and to another part of the world. It is not important
for us at present to decide whether the evidence Ignatius provides relates to Antioch, to Asia Minor, or to both. It is
important that we should remind ourselves that developments did not take place at the same speed, or even in the
same direction, in every part of the ancient world.

The only really new thing that we have to note in Ignatius
is that there is no longer any sort of equivalence between
presbyteros and *episkopos*; the two are sharply distinguished
and the bishop stands out as an isolated figure. References are
too numerous to be given in detail; a few examples must
suffice. Taking the letters in order we have *Ephesians* 4.1:[3] "It
becometh you to run in harmony with the mind of the bishop;
which thing also ye do. For your honourable presbytery,
which is worthy of God, is attuned to the bishop, even as its
strings to a lyre." 6.1: "Everyone whom the Master of the
household sendeth to be steward over His own house, we
ought so to receive as Him that sent him. Plainly therefore we
ought to regard the bishop as the Lord himself." *Magnesians*
contains a fully comprehensive picture. 6.1: "I advise you, be
ye zealous to do all things in godly concord, the bishop
presiding after the likeness of God and the presbyters after
the likeness of the council of the Apostles, with the deacons
also who are most dear to me, having been entrusted with the
diaconate of Jesus Christ (*diakonian Iēsou Christou*)". But all
was not well at Magnesia: "Some persons have the bishop's
name on their lips, but in everything act apart from him"
(4.1). The three orders appear side by side again in *Trallians*
2.2,3: "It is therefore necessary, even as your wont is, that ye
should do nothing without the bishop (*aneu tou episkopou*);
but be ye obedient also to the presbytery, as to the Apostles
of Jesus Christ our hope; for if we live in Him, we shall also
be found in Him. And those likewise who are deacons of the

See Note 2 on page 90

mysteries of Jesus Christ must please all men in all ways. For they are not deacons of meats and drinks but servants of the Church of God." In *Philadelphians pr.* Ignatius greets his readers, "more especially if they be at one with the bishop and the presbyters who are with him and with the deacons that have been appointed according to the mind of Jesus Christ." In *Smyrnaeans* the same theme is given a particular setting (7.2-8.2); "Shun divisions as the beginning of evils. Do ye all follow your bishop, as Jesus Christ followed the Father, and the presbytery as the Apostles; and to the deacons pay respect, as to God's commandment. Let no man do aught of things pertaining to the Church apart from the bishop. Let that be held a valid eucharist (*bebaia eucharistia*) which is under the bishop or one to whom he shall have committed it. Wheresoever the bishop shall appear, there let the people be; even as where [Christ] Jesus may be, there is the universal (*katholikē*) Church. It is not lawful (*exon*) without the bishop either to baptise or to hold a love-feast; but whatsoever he shall approve, this is well-pleasing also to God; that everything which ye do may be sure and valid (*asphales ēi kai bebaion*)". In the *Epistle to Bishop Polycarp* the same theme is heard in only slightly different terms. 1.2: "Vindicate thine office (*ekdikei sou ton topon*) in all diligence of flesh and of spirit." 5.2: "It becometh men and women, when they marry, to unite themselves with the consent of the bishop, that their marriage may be after the Lord and not after concupiscence." 6.1: "I am devoted to those who are subject to the bishop, the presbyters, the deacons". The one epistle that stands by itself is *Romans*; there is no allusion to a bishop of the Roman church, which we may suppose had not yet adopted the monarchical episcopate. If Ignatius had had reason to think that there was a single bishop in charge at Rome he would have referred to him even if he had not known his name.

What lay behind this remarkable development, which eventually affected the whole of ancient Christendom? A natural process of selection may have contributed to it. We have seen it to be probable that among the presbyters some stood out as being good at preaching and teaching and may have come to be called *episkopoi* (plural). Of these, perhaps, one stood out as the best at preaching and teaching and came to be known as **the** *episkopos* (singular). A theological analogy (of questionable validity) may have contributed: as Christ was to the apostles, so the bishop is to the presbyters. Ignatius, strikingly enough, does use divine language of the bishop. This suggestion, however, is not adequate for it leaves the deacons out of account, and Ignatius surprisingly does not follow Clement in his reference to the high priest, priests, and levites of the Old Testament. In the New Testament we come nearest to the Ignatian *monepiscopus* in the Presbyter and Diotrephes of 2 and 3 John; we need not doubt that a measure of *philoprōteuein*, of loving to have the first place, played its part in the development. Analogy with secular life and the social structure of cities and states also would play its part.

There is little to check or control the authoritarian atmosphere that was evidently developing. Polycarp is told to be firm and stand fast, and to speak to each man severally after the manner of God. If he is to care for widows, if he is bidden, "Bear all men, as the Lord also beareth thee. Suffer all men in love, as also thou doest" (*Polycarp* 1.2), these are rules for superior persons, rather than for those who know that as proclaimers of the Lord Jesus they can only be the slaves of their people (2 Cor. 4.5).

Like Clement, Ignatius uses sacrificial language. *Ephesians* 5.2: "If anyone be not within the precinct of the altar (*entos tou thysiastēriou*) he lacks the bread of God." Compare *Trallians* 7.2: "He that is within the sanctuary is clean; but he that is without the sanctuary is not clean, that is, he that doeth aught without the bishop and the presbytery and deacons, this man is not clean in his conscience." There seem to be thoughts here that Ignatius has not fully worked out. The reference to the bread of God can hardly fail to suggest the eucharist, and to provide it with a sacrificial context; but at the same time a general conception of church discipline, focused upon the church's hierarchy, is in mind. The relation between the eucharist and the hierarchical discipline is clear— see especially *Smyrnaeans* 8, quoted above; a eucharist is valid only if held by a bishop, or one (presumably a presbyter) appointed by him; but the conception of validity, of *bebaiotēs*, is extended to all churchly, indeed to all Christian, acts.

This theme of validity is one from which our final retrospect and summing up may start. We have travelled little more than sixty years from the earliest New Testament writings, but in that interval a good deal has happened.

The development of terminology, the increase in the number of labels available for Christian institutions, is not particularly important, though it bears witness to the process of Christian theologizing. We still lack the word *sacrament*, but we have *eucharist* as well as baptism and a quantity of sacrificial language. Any living institution, however, is sure to develop new terminology, which does not necessarily imply a changed or even a significantly developed structure. Since I played my last game of Rugby we have learned to speak of props, locks, number eights, flankers, and so on, but the game still looks much the same. The Pauline churches in the 40s and 50s were not without leaders, whether they bore titles or, like the household of Stephanas, simply saw a task to be done and set themselves (*etaxan heautous*) to do it.

Valid, *bebaios*, is not a new word, nor is it a new idea that something that Christians do may have lost its proper meaning and force. Christians in Corinth were coming together not for the better but for the worse (1 Cor. 11:17). This however was not because their eucharist or agape (the two have come to be separate in Ignatius's time; see *Smyrnaeans* 8:2, quoted above) was not held under the jurisdiction of a bishop; it was because each one was in such a hurry to get his own supper that it was impossible to eat the Lord's Supper. The rich were drunk, the poor were shamed; this was the ground of invalidity. It is not until later that we hear of the episcopal gifts and the ministry that authenticates them. All this is part of a quest for security, a flight from the dangerous *sola fide* of the New Testament. Christians came to feel, like most others in antiquity, that religion needed the visible, the tangible, if it was to be real and certain. It was no longer enough to look back to the ever more remote one sacrifice of the cross; gifts which God could see and the congregation could see must be offered too. It was no longer enough to present one's body to God in the living sacrifice of obedient faith.

There is a growing sense not only of the usefulness but of

the necessity of a ministry in the modern sense, consisting of persons distinguished from the main body of church members, able in virtue of their office to perform certain acts which are not permitted to the rest. Clement plainly models the Christian ministry on the Old Testament priesthood, without which the religious life, the essential life, of the people of God was not possible. As we have just reminded ourselves, Ignatius will have no baptism, eucharist, or agape without the bishop; indeed it is his approval that gives validity to any department of Christian life. To complete the quotation of *Smyrnaeans* 8:2 "Whatsoever he shall approve (*dokimasēi*), this is well-pleasing also to God (*kai tōi theōi areston*); that everything which ye do may be sure and valid (*asphales kai bebaion*)." We have come back to the theme of certainty and validity; and to the danger, now an imminent danger, that the church will so affirm itself and its own guaranteed validity as to destroy itself and the security of which Paul writes: "he who guarantees (*bebaiōn*) us, along with you, for Christ, and made us share his anointing, is God, who also sealed us, and in the Spirit put in our hearts the first instalment of our full blessedness" (2 Cor. 1:21,22).

The paragraphs I have just written should bring us back to another form of the paradox with which these lectures began. No one standing in my place, however much he may disagree with him in some matters, has any right to look down upon Ignatius, who, accompanied and chivvied by his ten leopards—a platoon of soldiers, who the better he treated them treated him the worse—was on his way to the real wild beasts of a Roman arena. He was a sincere Christian who loved his Lord, and the things by which such a man lived, in which he passionately believed, are worthy of respect. They are not, however, necessarily correct; only if one is to reject them, or any part of them, it is important to do so for the right reason. The church of Clement and Ignatius is what the church of Paul and John had developed into; and it is right, as we attempt to trace the development, to begin with the observation that the two have much in common. Let us attempt a brief list.

Of course, in each there is a personal devotion to the Lord Jesus Christ, regarded as the author of salvation, the one hope of the world. In each there is the conviction that he appeared on earth, truly man and in some sense truly God, in fulfilment of Old Testament Scripture, apart from which he could not be understood. In each it is recognized that he called and chose a group of apostles, and that he effected the salvation of the world by dying and rising from the dead. He will come again, and in the meantime the Holy Spirit guides those who believe in him. These constitute the church, and within this body there are certain leading figures, who preach the Gospel committed to them by Christ and perform other functions for the benefit of the whole community. The life of Christians is marked by faith, hope, and love. Initiates are baptized; the whole company meet to eat bread and drink wine together. They believe that after the death of the body God will raise them up.

This is a substantial body of agreement; it could be said that the ingredients of the mixture remain unchanged. But, as I have said, it is always important not only to have the right ingredients but also to know what to do with them. Different processes and combinations will result in different products. It is, I think, correct to say that most if not all of the ingredients of *Frühkatholizismus* (which we should now be able to recognise if not to define) are to be found in Paul and John; yet the product is not the same as in Clement and Ignatius (not to mention later representatives of the second-century church). Ministry; baptism; supper; authority; dogmatics; exclusiveness; readiness to come to terms with life in this world; these are all in the New Testament. Yet in comparison with what was later to emerge the product shows a subtle difference, not easy to define but, I think, impossible not to sense. Some things that at first seemed essential lose their point; others that seemed superfluous gain in importance. It is not only that the proportions of the mixture are different, though that is true and important. The continued extension of time was not only a matter of more of the same thing. After the first generation—does this mean the death of one whom we call the Beloved Disciple?—there was a real change. One could no longer look for an end speedy enough in itself to determine the present. There would be an end; it might come soon; but one did not know. Where is the promise of his coming? There was the threat of gnosis. This too was not quite new; it is implicit in Colossians; it is practically explicit in 1 John and the Pastorals. But a little later it was to get inside the Christian framework in a new and insidious way, and became, in various forms, including the Marcionite, the threat that the second-century church had to fight. And those religious and social pressures that I spoke of in the second lecture became heavier. Christianity was a religion; it must outdo the other religions. It could not afford to be less socially selective in its leadership than the secular society that surrounded it.

From the beginning Christians have lived in this world, and the various pressures I have referred to come from their living in this world as part of its history. What stands out when we move from the New Testament to the post-apostolic literature and the post-apostolic church is not so much the addition of something fresh as a deficiency in theological criticism, a theological criticism which is based upon the life, the crucifixion, and the resurrection of Jesus, and is capable of seeing that the church is most central in the purpose of God when it sees itself as merely peripheral. This theological criticism of religious and social forms and forces—a criticism as decisively and specifically Christian as the positive offer of righteousness and life in the Gospel—tended to decline, and other standards of criticism began to take its place. It was too easy to forget the words of Jesus about him who would be greatest in the Christian society; too easy to forget that those who proclaim Jesus as Lord must accept the corollary that they are the slaves of their people; too easy to forget that water is water, bread bread, and wine wine, whereas it is the Spirit that gives life; too easy to forget that it is better to give than to receive; above all, too easy to forget that being a disciple means taking up a cross and following in the steps of the Crucified. It is so easy to exercise power—for the good of others, of course; so natural to expect a return for one's labours—not necessarily a financial one, of course, but personal loyalty, respect, submission, and obedience; so comforting to think, I have been dipped in the water, I have eaten the bread, I have drunk the wine, and now I am secure; so good for the ego to say, My dogmatic presentation of the truth, and my form of the church, are the only permissible ones, and all the rest are wrong.

The church of every age is a building with glass walls and a glass roof, and it behoves us to be careful if we think of throwing stones at the second century; at least, men like Ignatius were readier for martyrdom than most of us for a modest degree of discomfort. But our topic in these lectures is Church, Ministry, and Sacraments in the New Testament, and if the church of the post-apostolic age points us back to the New Testament it sometimes does this in a somewhat backhanded way. And I find myself wondering whether the church in any age has taken the New Testament really seriously—seriously enough; whether we have learnt to balance our peripherality against our centrality; whether we believe that every member of the church is in some sense a minister and in every sense a priest, so that we do in honour prefer one another, encourage one another to find each his own ministry, and follow each his own calling for the good of all; whether every meal we take, especially every meal the church takes together, is transformed by the fact of the real presence; whether we honestly believe that it is better to give than to receive, to serve than to be served; whether we believe in the justifying gracious initiative of God, which looks for no desert whatever, and in his power to sanctify. It is these things, rather than any metaphysical—or antimeta-physical—*Weltanschauung* that must form the basis of our dogmatics, and these things rather than the pressure of our social environment or our charismatic enthusiasms that must determine the structures of church, ministry, and sacraments; because these things and these things alone constitute our present security and our future hope.

INDEXES

INDEX OF NEW TESTAMENT PASSAGES

OTHER EARLY CHRISTIAN LITERATURE

1 Clement

40:2-4		93
40:5		90
41:1		90
42:1-4		91
42:4,5		90
44:1-3		91
44:4		90, 93
44:5		90
47:1-3		90

Didache

9	62
11:11	56
11;12;13;15:1-2	44

Hermas
Vision II

4:3	45

Ignatius
Ephesians

4:1	94
6:1	94
20:2	74

Magnesians

4:1	94
6:1	94

Trallians

2:2	94
2:3	55, 94

Philadelphians

pr.	95

Smyrnaeans

7:2-8:2	95
8	96
8:2	97

Polycarp

1:2	95, 96
5:2	95
6:1	95

INDEX OF NAMES AND SUBJECTS

Index of Names and Subjects